EARLY TIMES ON THE SUSQUEHANNA.

EARLY TIMES

ON

THE SUSQUEHANNA.

BY

MRS. GEORGE A. PERKINS.

Fair river, though thus silently you flow,
On thy green banks once woke the wail of woe.
Lewers.

BINGHAMTON:
MALETTE & REID, PRINTERS,
1870.

A Facsimile Reprint
Published 1999 by

HERITAGE BOOKS, INC.
1540E Pointer Ridge Place
Bowie, Maryland 20716
1-800-398-7709
www.heritagebooks.com

ISBN 0-7884-1298-1

INTRODUCTION.

A MEETING of the early settlers of this region was held at Athens, Pa., in the Presbyterian church, on the 22d of February, 1854.

The venerable Major Flower, a Revolutionary soldier, and long known as an efficient surveyor, was called to the chair, sustained by Hon. Dr. Barstow of Nichols, and Hon. H. Williston of Athens, as Vice-Presidents.

Many ancient men, and a large number of the descendants of the first settlers were present, and were highly entertained by addresses from Dr. Barstow, Judge Williston, Hon. Thomas Maxwell of Elmira, Judge Avery of Owego, Judge McDowell of Chemung, and others. There were representatives from Owego, Elmira, and the neighboring towns, some of whom gave historical sketches of their respective districts.

Dr. Barstow opened the meeting, stating the object for which they had assembled, and called attention to the importance of collecting facts and incidents connected with the early settlement of the country. He thought it highly proper that we should know the history of the first settlement of our country.

Hon. C. P. Avery, who was called upon, commenced his remarks by exhibiting the original Indian title or conveyance of a tract of land, made by the Indians to Amos Draper, the first white settler at Owego. This tract was three miles in width, and six in length, including the site of the present village of Owego. It is written in the Iroquois language, said to be far the most beautiful of any Indian language, but now extinct. Judge Avery had procured a translation, through a learned Seneca Chief,* which he read. It had been recently found among some old papers in the garret of one of the descendants of Mr. Draper.

It was passed through the assembly, exciting great interest, and was looked upon as a rare and valuable curiosity. He proceeded to give a graphic history of Owego and the neighboring towns,—Nichols, Barton, Berkshire, Candor, and Spencer,—from their early settlement by the white people, and the names of the Pioneers who first settled these places.

Hon. Thomas Maxwell confined his remarks principally to Tioga Point, and cherished a warm regard for the village of his birth and the scenes of his early childhood, and while life and health were spared, would be ready to contribute to the preservation of the history of the first settlement of our beautiful valley.

Judge Williston made a striking comparison between

* Mr. E. S. Parker.

the state of the country fifty years ago when he was passing down from Broome County to Bradford, along the
valley. Then the improvements were comparatively new.
There were two skeletons of churches, and two or three
school-houses. Now the entire distance is covered with
villages, churches, academies, school-houses, and highly
cultivated farms. Judge Williston always showed himselт
the friend of the early Connecticut settler, and referred to
the Trenton Decree, and the difficulty of procuring title to
the lands, as greatly retarding the settlement of the country.

Judge McDowell thought we should visit and converse
with the few that yet remain of the early settlers, and
gather all the historical facts about early times that could
be obtained. He hoped a minute and accurate history
would soon be written.

Such meetings of the early settlers have doubtless had a
salutary influence among the descendants of the early
Pioneers, perpetuating and cementing the bond of union
which originated with their fathers in the days of their
privations and hardships, when their sympathies were mutual. The first of these gatherings was held at Elmira in
1853, the second at Athens, 1854, and the third at Owego,
1855. It was affecting to observe how rapidly these aged
veterans passed away from one of the "Old Settlers' meetings," to another. The deaths of many familiar friends

were reported from year to year, and the number has continued to diminish rapidly, until it is difficult to find one, whose faculties of mind and body are not too much impaired to be able to communicate intelligently. Hence the embarrassment of furnishing a complete history.

At the close of the meeting first mentioned, Judge Avery urged it as the duty of some resident to write the history of this place and vicinity. Fifteen years have passed, and no such looked-for record has appeared. Having some facilities from my late father's papers, in my possession, I propose for the benefit of my children and others who may feel an interest in the subject, to make such statements as these documents, together with information received from my ancestors, and from authors whom I have consulted, and my own personal knowledge, may enable me to do.

I would also gratefully acknowledge the kindness of friends who have aided me in the work.

It is natural for the intelligent to wish to learn all they can about the history of their ancestors, and the place of their own nativity; and if this sketch can afford any gratification to the living, or be useful to those who may come after, the object will be accomplished.

CONTENTS.

EARLY TIMES.

I

INDIANS.

LARGE and powerful tribes of Indians inhabited the territories of New York, New Jersey and Pennsylvania less than a hundred years ago. The Delawares, or Lenni Lenape, whose sub-divisions were numerous, some of them known as the Turtle, the Turkey and the Wolf tribes, had been the most powerful, until the Five Nations formed a league to subjugate and make them vassals. This they did most effectually early in the 18th century, and ever after treated them as subjects.

The five confederate nations were the Mohawks, Oneidas, Onondagas, Cayugas and Senecas. Historians speak of the Tuscaroras, as having been driven from North Carolina and adopted by the confederates at a later period, constituting, with them, the Six Nations, and called by the French, Iroquois, and by the English Mingoes.

The Monsey or Wolf tribe, a part of the Delawares, was powerful and warlike, and occupied both branches of the Susquehanna. The Shamokins, Shawnees and Nanticokes, also were powerful, but these were all subject to the great confederacy, the Six Nations, and nothing could exceed the severity with which they treated those who dared to transgress their code ; to take the liberty to sell land, or to attempt to rise above their degradation. It was jealousy of the growing popularity of Tedeu'scung, the Delaware chief, among the white people, that instigated that barbarous act of a party of warriors from the Six Nations when they visited Wyoming upon a pretence of friendship, but one night set fire to the house of the chief, together with which he was burned to ashes. He was a man of ability, and his death was greatly lamented. The Delawares had no name or place except such as was granted them by their merciless conquerors. They cowered before their powerful foe. In this subdued state perhaps they were the better prepared to receive the gospel, when it was proclaimed to them. They called themselves the original people, and their language was the Algonquin.

Count Zinzendorf, Zeisberger and others amo. the Moravians, labored among them at a very early date. David and John Brainard, New England missionaries, were received among the Delawares of New Jersey, as friends of the red man, and it is astonishing to note the access these men had to the hearts of these degraded people, some of them only able to address them through an interpreter.

In many cases powerful revivals of religion were known among them, and many of the converts became consistent Christians, and continued steadfast through life.

After the Six Nations had subjugated the Delawares, or, as they expressed it, "clothed them in petticoats," they soon commenced their emigration down the beautiful valley to their newly acquired territories. Tioga Point was doubtless the rallying place for many a stately Indian, clothed in his blanket or skins, attended by his squaw and papooses, migrating south in his Indian canoe, to take possession of his conquered domain, and enjoy the pleasures and benefits of his incomparable hunting and fishing ground.

The Delawares received them with kindness; they dared not do otherwise, and their good Christian teachers, who had great influence with them, taught them to bear their trials patiently, and to recommend religion to their enemies by their lives and conversation. This was not without its effect. We read that many among the confederates embraced the Christian religion.

Mr. Maginnes speaks of Shikelimy, a chief of the Cayuga tribe, who was stationed at Shamokin, to rule over the Indians. He was an excellent man, possessed of many noble qualities of mind, that would do honor to many a white man laying claims to greater refinement and intelli-

gence. He was possessed of great dignity, sobriety
and prudence, and was particularly noted for his
kindness to the whites and missionaries. He was
a most intimate and valued friend of Conrad
Weiser, agent for the government, and interpreter,
who entertained great respect for him. On several
important occasions he attended the sittings of the
Provincial Council at Philadelphia, and performed many embassies between the government of
Pennsylvania and the Six Nations. He was the
first magistrate and head Chief of all the Iroquois
Indians living on the banks of the Susquehanna,
and as far as Onondaga. He had several sons, one
of whom was "Logan, the Mingo Chief."

He became a convert to Christianity, and in his
last illness was attended by David Zeisberger, and
in his presence died a peaceful and happy death,
with full assurance of eternal life through the
merits of Jesus Christ.

Governor Hamilton, of Pennsylvania, sent to
condole with his family after his death, and presents were given them, in order to wipe away their
tears. The presents were matchcoats, shirts and a
string of wampum.

The Indians of our country have ever been
looked upon with interest by every lover of history. They have justly been charged with savage
cruelties, such as make the blood chill, when
called to mind. But when we look upon them as
natives of the soil, and we the invaders ; when we
consider how all nations are affected by intrusion
and oppression, and what excesses of barbarity the
most civilized nations have allowed and prac-

ticed ; we might do well to extend charity to the less cultivated and refined, who have not had the advantages with which we have been favored.

Those who have felt an interest in them, and studied their character, and those who have spent months and years among them, instructing them in civilization and Christianity, are not backward in ascribing to them the characteristics of humanity, common to the fallen race of Adam, and it has been proved, in very many instances, where their minds have been instructed and their hearts renewed by Divine grace, that they have been among the most humane, sensible and reliable of men.

The white man who indulges in deeds of cruelty acts contrary to the laws of civilized society ; not so with the Indian in his savage state ; he is consistent with his principles, and conducts accordingly.

After the labors of the Brainards and Tennents had closed in New Jersey, and the Moravian Indians had removed West, no one was found to guide them. Some of them had received instruction at the school for Indian youth, at Lebanon, Conn., under the care of the Rev. Mr. Wheelock, founder of Dartmouth College. But they were not competent to direct the minds of the people, and they suffered much from ignorance and neglect. Cruel men took the advantage of them, acting upon the principle that the "Indian had no rights which white men were bound to respect." In 1802 many of them resolved to go to the Oneidas, on Oneida Lake, who had invited them to "eat of their dish," saying it was large enough for both.

The united tribes remained there until 1824, when the encroachments of the whites induced them to purchase a tract of land on Fox river, near Green Bay.

The few that remained in New Jersey applied by memorial to the Legislature of the State, for compensation for their claim, through Bartholomew Calvin, an educated Chief, 76 years old. He had been in Princeton College, until the Revolutionary war cut off the funds of the society, by which he was supported. He afterward taught school when he had as many white as Indian pupils.

In his petition to the Legislature he says, "my brethren I am old, and weak, and poor, and therefore a fit representative of my people. You are young, and strong, and rich, and therefore a fit representative of your people. But let me beg you for a moment to lay aside the recollection of your strength, and our weakness, that your minds may be prepared to examine with candor, the subject of our claim." Then stating their claim, he says, "we consider the State Legislature the proper purchaser, and trust that you will be induced to give us what you deem a proper compensation. In behalf of the Red brethren —Bartholomew Calvin."

The Legislature granted him two thousand dollars on his petition. He returned his thanks to both Houses, in the name of "a wasted yet grateful people."

Some now living may remember the final departure of the Delaware Indians for their new home among the Oneidas ; their scanty furniture, their rude relics, the aged, the sick, and the little ones, which were packed in wagons while the healthy marched on foot, and some were playing on the violin to cheer up the desponding. They became amalgamated with the Oneidas, and were soon mingling with the white inhabitants, selling their split brooms and baskets.

In 1830 the Oneidas sold much of their land to the State ; many remaining still on their reservation ; yet in 1832 most of these tribes migrated to Green Bay. They .have since gone still farther west. Mr. Marsh the missionary says : "I have met with several of the children of David Brainard's people, and obtained of one of them the conch shell with which Brainard used to call the people together for public worship, in New Jersey. Some of them pray in their families, dress well, and behave well." What did your grandmother say about David Brainard, Mr. M. inquired of one of them. She said, "He was a young man—a lovely man, he was a staff to walk with. He went from house to house, to talk about religion—that was his way."

Skanadoah, an Oneida Chief, and a convert to the Christian religion, died in 1815, aged about 113 years. He had been a pupil of Mr. Kirkland, the missionary who labored about forty years for the benefit of the Oneidas. Mr. Kirkland donated the land for Hamilton College, and it is said that through him and Dr. Wheelock, both Hamilton and Dartmouth Colleges arose indirectly as the result of Indian missions. Mr. K. lived at Oneida Castle, with his family. He died at Clinton in

1808, aged 66 years. Skanadoah was buried at his particular request by the side of the missionary, to whom he had been much attached. A monument was erected to him, by the corporation of Hamilton College, within the College burying ground.

He is represented by a poet as saying at his death:

> "Lo! my war shout is ended, my bow is unstrung
> And warriors! I rise to the hills of my rest,
> I meet not your feasts, and I meet not your song,
> There's a home for the Chief in the isles of the blest."

The Six Nations had great power in the territory of Pennsylvania, until they sold to the white people. Their fishing and hunting grounds, in these wilds, were unequaled. The shad, the bass, and the trout, the bear, the stately elk, and herds of deer gave them business, food and clothing, and with their variety of corn dishes, their fare was good and wholesome. Their councils were numerous, where they repeated their legends, and handed down the traditions of former ages, to be again repeated to those who should come after them. At these councils their women were not only allowed to be present, but their opinions were consulted in war debates, and strange to say of heathen, their women often acted as mediators, and when they advised to lay down the hatchet, their arguments often prevailed.

But labor was principally confined to the women, and it was deemed disgraceful for a man to work. Even as late as 1831, a missionary among the Sene-

cas at Cattaraugus states that a man might hunt
and fish and play ball and fight, and maintain his re-
spectability, but he could not even bring his game
into the settlement. Suppose he had been out into
the Pennsylvania forests, and killed a deer, he
might bring it all the way on his shoulders, 'till
he came within a mile of the settlement ; but "eti-
quette" required him to leave it there, and go
home, and say to the women, "In such a place
you will find some vension which I have brought
you," and they must go out and lug it into
camp.

The Oneidas and Senecas were set to guard the
subjugated tribes along the branches of the Susquehanna. They separated the Nanticokes, plac-
ing a portion of them north, near Owego, and
some of them down the valley below Wilkesbarre. The Delawares were scattered, to weaken
their power, and the other tribes placed here
and there, at the discretion of their lordly conquerors. The Monsey or Wolf tribe, were very
warlike, and were likewise separated, some
placed on the West Branch, near Monsey, others
below Tioga Point, where they had a village
called Wilawane, or Monseytown. They removed
west in Pennsylvania to Venango. Queen Esther's
village was afterwards built upon the same ground
along on the ridge.

Among the Six Nations there were many distinguished men. Some noted for their talents, and
others for their cruelty. Shickeleny has been
spoken of as a man of noble mind and a Christian ; Brant, a Mohawk chief, possessed superior

talents, had received some education, and was a
"British officer in epaulets;" * Canassitigo, an
Onondaga chief, so cruel and sarcastic towards the Delawares, (an account of which
may be found in Miner's History of Wyoming);
the good and talented Skanadoah, of the Oneidas; and Cornplanter, a Seneca chief, and
friend of the white man, who was well-known
in his prime by the whites and Indians on
the West and North branches of the Susquehanna, and did much to conciliate, in cases of
difficulty. In later life he lived on a small reservation in Pennsylvania, about four miles below
the State line, on the Allegany river. He died a
little more than thirty years ago. A neat and
tasteful monument was erected over his grave, in
1866, at the expense of the state of Pennsylvania.
He was supposed to be about 107 years of age.
Missionaries who have long labored in that reservation speak well of his family. He has two sons
and a daughter still living, and numerous grandchildren. Red Jacket, another Seneca chief, was
perhaps, better known in New York and Northern Pennsylvania than any other chief. He vis-
ted Tioga Point many times, and figured largely
at the treaty in 1790. His powers of eloquence
were said to be very great. Some now living here
remember him. He lived on the reservation near
Buffalo, and died in about 1830. Many others,

---

* Colonel Parker, the well-known Seneca Indian gentleman, on
General Grant's staff during the late war, states that Brant was the
translator of the gospel into Iroquois. Colonel Stone corroborates
his statement in his life of Brant.

whose names will appear in the account of the treaty, were noted and influential men.

It is well understood that the valley we now occupy was once inhabited by these Indian tribes, principally Senecas, Cayugas and Oneidas, their headquarters being at Onondaga. This valley was the grand thoroughfare from that place to Wyoming, and still further south.

These rivers and mountains, these plains and valleys, islands and grottoes were as familiar to them as they are to us. They owned the soil, and tilled it with their rude implements. Their Indian corn grew where much of ours now grows. They here took from these rivers the fish, the "delicious shad," which we once enjoyed, but from which we are now cut off by our *improvements*. They sailed on these waters, in their native canoes. With their bow and arrow they caught the bounding deer of the forest, his flesh was their food, and his skin their clothing. Their council fires were kindled on the banks of the Susquehanna; they smoked the pipe of peace under these lofty elms; they bathed in these rivers; their lovers walked on these banks, and made their plans for future life. They knew of no superiors, and were subject to no dictation but their great council at Onondaga.

They engaged in the old French war against the English, and were powerful foes. But they had been invaders upon the Delawares, and now a stronger nation was crowding them out of their possessions. Purchases of lands were made of them by the white people, at very low prices, at various times, which weakened their power, and soured their minds, and when the Revolutionary war was in progress, the most of the tribes were readily engaged on the British side, against the colonies ; the Oneidas for the most part being our faithful friends, throughout the conflict. It is wonderful that the colonists should ever have attained their independence, with the British on their front, the Indians on their rear, and the tories in their midst ; the interposition of Divine Providence was manifest, and His agency was gratefully acknowledged by the Commander-in-Chief.

It was about this time of their power and pride, that the Indians were instigated by the British to engage with them in their murderous expedition into Wyoming Valley, to deprive the inhabitants of their fathers, brothers and possessions, and put the distressed families to flight. But vengeance pursued them, and in a short time they were driven into close and uncomfortable quarters, in their own possessions, or compelled to find uncertain homes among their British friends in Canada. *

---

* These accounts of the Indians are gathered principally from the several histories of Wyoming, the lives of John and David Brainard, and the Moravian papers.

II

MORAVIAN MISSIONS--WYALUSING.

THE first account we have of the labors of the Moravian Brethren among the Indians of Pennsylvania, is from their own history. They commenced their missions in 1740 ; one in the State of New York. the other in Connecticut, twenty miles distant, under the care of Rev. Martin Mack, and were very successful in instructing them in the Christian religion. But they were so persecuted by the white people, that after four years the "Brethren" thought best to remove them, forty in number, to Bethlehem for protection, where they built huts for themselves, and called their settlement Friedenshuetten, or Tents of Peace. Their numbers increased so much that in a few months the Brethren bought a tract of land for them, near the Mahony creek, and the Lehigh river.

Their missionary and others laid out the town, which they called Gnadenheutten, or Tents of Grace. They soon numbered five hundred Indians.

The war between the French and English commenced in 1755. The Christian Indians were friends to the British, while the savages were engaged for the French.

The French Indians threatened the Christian Indians, and were a constant terror to them. At last they attacked the mission house on the Mahony one evening, and eleven of the inhabitants were murdered. Application was made to Governor Denny for protection. They were removed to the barracks in Philadelphia, where fifty-five of them died. They were buried in what is now Washington Square.

After the close of the French war, in 1764, the troubles being nearly at an end, the Brethren in Bethlehem considered in what manner to provide a settlement for these poor Indians, principally Delawares, where they might enjoy more safety.

It could not be expected they would remain long unmolested, in the neighborhood of the merciless whites, and they were therefore advised to settle in the Indian country, on the banks of the Susquehanna. Application was made to the Governor, who gave them permission, and supplied them liberally with necessaries "until their new planted corn should ripen." Schmidt and Zeisberger were appointed to accompany them. On the 20th of March the Moravian Indian congregation commenced their journey across the mountains, and swamps, direct to Wyoming; from thence to Machiwilusing, where they arrived on the 9th of May, after a painful pilgrimage of five weeks.

Machiwilusing was the Indian name for Wyalusing creek, and has given name to the town. It empties into the Susquehanna, a little below French Town, on the opposite side of the river. Near the mouth of that creek, these Moravians made their missionary establishment in 1765. They called it after their old station Friedenshuetten or Tents of Peace. It was a village of forty houses, built of wood, after the European manner, and thirteen Indian huts. In the middle of the street, which was eighty feet broad, they built a large and neat chapel. The adjoining ground was laid out in gardens, and between the town and the river, about 250 acres were divided into regular plantations, for Indian corn. The burying ground was situated some distance back of the buildings. The mission grounds were about two miles below the present village of Wyalusing.

They were happy and greatly blessed, and prospered, at their new station, and were often visited by people of the Six Nations, many of whom believed the word which they heard, and embraced their religion, and were baptised. The natives heard of them at a great distance, and great numbers were added to them.

Zeisberger was extensively known among the Indians. He understood the Delaware and Iroquois languages, and often attended the great councils at Onondaga, where he was treated with great respect. They gave him not only liberty to settle at Friedenshuetten, but additional liberties beyond Tioga. *

Among other places visited by the missionaries of Machiwilusing, was a town about thirty miles up the river called She Shequanunck (Old Sheshequin) in which a great awakening took place

---

* We have no account of the Moravions having gone farther North than old Sheshequin.

among the Indians, occasioned by the accounts from Friedenshuetten, brought by those who visited them. At the request of the natives, the missionary Rothe went to reside among them. His testimony of Jesus went to their hearts, the audience being frequently melted into tears. One of them remarked "I would not have wept if my enemies had cut the flesh from my bones. That I now weep is of God, who has softened the hardness of my heart." For some time it appeared as if the whole town would turn to the Lord and be converted.

The mission at Machiwilusing continued to prosper greatly until the whites increased on each side of them, and introduced rum. The difficulties also among the Pennsylvania and New England people were a hindrance to them, and the Iroquois were prevailed upon to sell all their lands East of the Ohio to the white people, and great was the sacrifice to give up their beautiful settlement on the Susquehanna. These peaceable, quiet, christian Moravian Indians felt compelled to leave their "Tents of Peace" where they had lived seven years, and take up their march again westward, by the way of Sunbury, through forest and marshes, over rivers and mountains, till they arrived on the banks of the Ohio, where they met brethren under Heckwalder, the Moravian missionary, who guided them to their settlement. These poor creatures (two hundred and forty in number), were seven weeks on their sad journey.

A Congregational church was formed in Wyalusing in 1794, and was connected with the Luzerne

Association. Rev. M. M. York preached alternately at Wyalusing and Wysox, for many years. The Association once met at the latter place, in the spring of ——, when Mrs. York, the mother of the clergyman, more than seventy years of age, residing at Wyalusing, rode across swollen streams and over dangerous passes, to be present at this assembly. Great surprise was expressed at her courage and heroism, when she replied, "I have been praying forty years for the upbuilding of Zion, and don't you think I would come to see it."

Major Taylor's family were identified with the church there, and a son of his was a clergyman. His daughter was suddenly restored to the use of her limbs, in answer to prayer, as was supposed, after having been unable to walk for several years.

A settlement was made by the white people, soon after the close of the Revolutionary war, which they called Wyalusing, from Mackhiwilusing, the Indian name of the Creek.

It is a beautiful settlement, about two miles above the site of the old Moravian Settlement, and contained a population of nearly five hundred inhabitants.

The late C. F. Welles, Esq., removed from Towanda to Wyalusing in 1822. He had been the Prothonotary, and Register and Recorder of Bradford county, from the time its name was changed from that of Ontario, March 24, 1812, until 1818, when he was succeeded by Geo. Scott and E. Mason.

He married a daughter of Judge Hollenback.

and was a prominent and talented man. He died in 1866. *

* Justus Lewis, Esq., who resides near Wyalusing, and is about 82 years of age, has a better knowledge, it is said, of our frontier history, than any other man now living, and could no doubt give valuable information to any one who might wish to prepare a more extended work.

III.

CONNECTICUT TITLE.

TO take a glance of the two states of Connecticut and Pennsylvania, as they now are, it might seem absurd that Connecticut could ever have claimed a tract of land over one hundred and twenty miles in length, and sixty in breadth, in the heart of this well proportioned state.

The Colony of Connecticut claimed jurisdiction by virtue of a charter from Charles 2nd, dated April 23, 1662, granting Connecticut that part of his dominions in America, beginning at Narragansett Bay, from the 41st to the 42d degree of latitude, in width, and extending west on the same parallels of latitude, so far as England then owned the granting power, or as some say to the Pacific Ocean, supposing the Continent to be very narrow. The claims of the Dutch leading down to New York Bay, were, of course, excepted, as her charter was the oldest.

The proprietaries of Pennsylvania, on the ground of a charter granted to Wm. Penn, in 1681, by the same sovereign, claimed all that tract of land in America, bounded on the east by the Delaware river, from the 40th to the 42d degree of north latitude,

and to extend west through five degrees of longitude.
Within these bounds was included Wyoming,
"which," says Colonel Stone, "has been the
theatre of more historical action, and is invested
with more historical interest than any other inland
district of the United States, of equal extent."

The difficulties arising out of these opposing
claims, between Connecticut and Pennsylvania,
were serious and protracted. It was inexcusable
that a monarch, assigning portions of territory to
his subjects, should leave so much ground for
controversy, by granting titles that conflicted with
each other to so great an extent.

It was this that caused the trouble between the
two states and the numerous claimants, and resulted in civil and disastrous wars.

Pennsylvania purchased of the Indians the right
of soil in the province, but did not receive their
deed until the treaty at Fort Stanwix, in 1768.

In 1754 the Connecticut Susquehanna Company,
formed at Hartford, purchased of the Six Nations,
at Albany, the land on the Susquehanna river, beginning at the 41st degree of North latitude, ten
miles east of the river ; and from thence, with a
northerly line, following the river ten miles east of
the same, to the forty-second degree of North latitude ; and extending two degrees West longitude ;
from thence south to the 41st degree ; thence east
to the first mentioned boundary.

For this the Company paid the Indians the sum
of two thousand pounds, current money, and the
deed was signed by eighteen Sachems. *

* See Miner's history.

A gradual emigration was in progress from Connecticut many years, though interrupted considerably by the French war ; but in 1769 two hundred families, from the eastern part of the State, formed a colony and began to remove to the south part of the valley, with ministers, and implements of husbandry, and teachers for their children. After many wearisome days in the wilderness, they descended the mountain and took possession of that garden of nature, which had been honorably purchased of the natives.

Here, in their delightful Wyoming, these noble Christian colonists expected to find a prosperous and peaceful home. But scarcely had they taken possession, when their claim was contested by the Pennsylvanians, whose charter also covered the charming valley ; and a terrible conflict ensued. The contention was long and sharp ; many lives were lost, and the sufferings of the colony were great. At three different times they were driven from their possessions by the Pennsylvanians ; but they returned with increased numbers, supported by Connecticut, and established themselves strongly. They called their territory the County of Westmoreland, and for nine years sent representatives to the Legislature of Connecticut. They were a happy people among themselves, had civil and religious privileges, and all the enjoyments of refined social life. Their Puritan habits have blessed succeeding generations. Many clergymen, statesmen, teachers, missionaries, and other eminent Christian men and women, have sprung from this stock.

Chief-Justice Tilghman states that "the unfortunate controversy between Connecticut and Pennsylvania was attended with riot, disorder and bloodshed, which continued until the commencement of the Revolutionary war, when the Congress of the United States, fearing the consequences which might result from a dispute of so serious a nature between two powerful States, recommended that all acts of force should be abstained from, and each person should remain in possession of the land occupied by him, until a proper season should come for determining the matter on principles of justice. This recommendation was complied with. The Connecticut settlers were the most numerous, and held possession during the war, in the course of which they suffered great hardships, and lost many lives ; being on a remote frontier, much exposed to the attacks of the British and Indians."*

While the struggle with Great Britain was in progress, in which Wyoming took an active part, there was comparative quiet between the Connecticut and Pennsylvania claimants ; but scarcely was our independence acknowledged, when the contention about lands revived. It was found necessary that a subject of so much weight should be decided by a court established by Congress of

---

* The fiery trials through which they passed, at the time of the invasion by the Tories and Indians, in 1778, cannot be better described than in the petition of Samuel Gore, for a pension, in his advanced age. He was a brother of Judge Gore, and kindly presented me with a copy of his petition, written with his own hand, near the close of his life. He had often visited us, and entertained us with his account of the Revolutionary war, and the battle of Wyoming.

Commissioners from the two contending states. They met at Trenton, N. J., in the month of December, 1782. The parties proceeded with their pleas, and after many days the court decided that the right of jurisdiction belonged to Pennsylvania, and that the judicial power of Connecticut over Wyoming should cease. In this the Commissioners from each state acquiesced. It is supposed there was this understanding between the two states, from a conviction of its policy.

Mr. Miner says, "there is no doubt that the decision of Trenton was made on grounds of *policy*, and not of *right*. It was not designed, however, to affect the private right of soil. Immediately after this decree, Connecticut withdrew its jurisdiction, and the county of Westmoreland ceased to exist.

"The claims of Connecticut, west of Pennsylvania, were all ceded to Congress, excepting the Western Reserve, or New Connecticut, and she received the United States letters patent for that tract."

"The Pennsylvanians continued to treat the Connecticut settlers with severity, which induced the Assembly to pass an act, to restore to them the possessions from which they had been forcibly removed. On the 28th of March, 1787, an act was passed called the *Confirming Act*, ratifying the title of lands in their possession, prior to the decree of Trenton.

This law was not satisfactory to either party, and was repealed April 1st, 1790. On the 4th of April, 1799, an act was passed called the Compromising Act, "offering compensation to the Pennsylvania settlers, within the seventeen townships of Luzerne. The object of this act was to offer a reasonable compensation in money to such Pennsylvania claimants as were willing to release their rights, in order that the Commonwealth, having thus regained the title, might confirm the estates of the Connecticut settlers, at a moderate price, fixed by Commissioners, who were authorized to give certificates to Connecticut claimants for no other land than such as may have been released by the Pennsylvania claimants. This title was confirmed by paying for first-class lands two dollars per acre ; second-class, one dollar and twenty cents ; third-class, fifty cents ; fourth-class, eight and one-quarter cents.

To induce the Pennsylvania claimants to release, the Commissioners were authorized to classify the land, giving certificates to them ; first-class lands to be paid for at the rate of five dollars per acre, etc.

On the 6th of April, 1802, a supplement was passed to the act of 1799, which gave to the Commissioners authority to certify to Connecticut claimants the title to their lands, whether released by the Pennsylvania claimant or not ; forbidding recovery of the lands by the Pennsylvania claimant, and giving him a right of action against the Commonwealth for the value of his land.

By the act of 1807, all Pennsylvania claimants were admitted who had acquired title prior to the first confirming law, of March, 1787, and Connecticut claimants were not required to show that the lands were occupied before the decree of Trenton. In the case of Mrs. Mathewson in the contest with J. F. Satterlee, Mrs. M. had taken out a warrant in 1812, and claimed an improvement back to 1785, under Connecticut title, (she having no certificate from the Commissioners,) and therefore had no title recognized by the laws of Pennsylvania to the date of her warrant, (1812.) Mr. Satterlee had purchased an old Pennsylvania title, going back to 1769, and had taken a lease of Mrs. Mathewson, after which an act of Assembly was passed, which allowed Mrs. M. to hold him as tenant. The same principles, when applied, will explain other cases also.*

THE PETITION OF SAMUEL GORE, ESQ.

"JANUARY, 1832.

" *To the Honorable the Senate and House of Representatives of the United States, in Congress assembled, at the City of Washington :*

"The petition and memorial of Samuel Gore, of Sheshequin Township, Bradford County, Pennsylvania, humbly showeth :

"That your petitioner's request is of a singular nature, differing from the common case of those who served in the War of the Revolution ; was not engaged for any limited time ; that he resided at

------

* The above statements have been furnished by a legal gentleman for this work.

Wyoming Settlement at the commencement of the late Revolutionary War ; that in the year 1777, in the month of May, he was enrolled in the militia of Captain Aholiab Buck's company, and took the oath of allegiance, to be true and faithful to the cause then at issue ; that in December, the same year, he was draughted on a tour of duty up the river, as far as Wysox and Towanda ; the command he was attached to took twenty-eight prisoners, men that had served under General Burgoyne, the preceding campaign ; that in the year 1778 the Settlement was in almost continual alarm, the fore part of the season ; and what added mostly to our fears was, that three companies of soldiers had been enlisted in the Settlement, and had joined the main army of Washington.

"The militia that was left was on duty the principal part of the time, in fortifying, scouting, and learning the military discipline, till the month of July, when the settlement was invaded by the British and Indians, under the command of Colonel John Butler and Brandt, the Indian Chief.

"Your petitioner was in the memorable battle and massacre of Wyoming, and narrowly escaped the fate of five brethren, the officers, and principal part of the Company to which he belonged.

"In addition to his misfortune, in running across a bay or morass, the Indians in close pursuit, every step over the knee in mud and mire, by over exertion, caused a breach in his body, which has been a painful and troublesome disorder ever since.

"It is unnecessary to describe the entire destruction of the settlement, by the enemy, the dispersions and hardships of the fugitives. Old men, women and children, · fleeing through the wilderness, carrying with them scarcely enough to support nature by the way.

"The place was retaken in August or September following, by Colonel Zebulon Butler and Captain Simon Spalding, and a garrison replaced there. Your petioner returned soon after, and served as a volunteer, during the years of 1779, 1780 and 1781, and was subject to be called on, in every case of emergency.

"The expedition of General Sullivan to the Gennesse country, did not prevent wholly, the depredations of the enemy, being frequently harassed by small parties. In the year 1782 Captain Spalding's company was called to join the main army, at headquarters, and a company of invalids was stationed at the post, commanded by a Captain Mitchel, soldiers that were not calculated for the woods, scouting, etc. Colonel Dennison gave orders to have the militia organized and classed, which took place.

"John Franklin was chosen Captain. Your petitioner was appointed a Sergeant, and had the command of a class, which was ordered to be ready at the shortest notice, to scout the woods, and to follow any party of the enemy that should be sent on their murderous excursions. That he performed four tours of scouting that season, of about eight days each.

"Your petitioner never drew any pay, clothing or rations, during the contest for Independence, but ammunition, he was supplied with from the continental store.

" Had the charge of the family at the time, (his father being dead); had to support himself as well as he could, by laboring between spells, and frequently ploughing with his musket slung at his back.

" Being informed by the newspapers, that a bill has passed the House of Representatives, by a large majority, to compensate all those that were enlisted in the service of their country from three months to six, and nine; to compensate according to the time of their engagement, let their circumstances be what they may. Encouraged by the liberality and generosity of our National legislators, I take the liberty to request of your Honorable Body, to take my case into consideration; and if you, in your wisdom and justice, should think that your petitioner is entitled to any remuneration, to do what you may think right and just; and your petitioner will ever pray."

A letter addressed to Philander Stephens, Esq., a Member of Congress, was folded within the petition, which I also copy:

"SHESHEQUIN, April 3, 1832.
"PHILANDER STEPHENS, Esq.—Dear Sir: I have been waiting with considerable anxiety, for some time, expecting to hear from you, as I think you promised to write to me. I would take it as a favor, if you would inform me what is the prospect of the bill for the general compensation of old soldiers and volunteers of the Revolution; whether

it is like to pass the Senate, the present session ;
also whether you have presented my petition, and
if any encouragement therefrom. Some cheering
information on this subject would revive my
spirits, which have been almost exhausted during
the severity of the past winter—the hardest I have
experienced since the return of Sullivan's expedition to the Indian country, in the year 1779.

"On reflecting back in these trying times, I
would state some particulars respecting our family,
at the commencement of the Revolution. My
father had seven sons, all zealously engaged in
the cause of liberty. Himself an acting magistrate, and a committee of safety, watching the dis-
affected and encouraging the loyal part of the
community.

"Three of his sons, and two sons-in-law, fell in
the Wyoming massacre. Himself died the winter
following. One son served during the war, the
others served in the Continental army for shorter
periods.

" Let any person at this time of general prosperity
of our country, reflect back on the troubles, trials
and suffering of a conquered country by a savage
enemy. Men scalped and mangled in the most
savage manner. Some dead bodies floating down
the river in sight of the garrison. Women collecting together in groups, screaming and wringing
their hands, in the greatest agony ; some swoon-
ing and deprived of their senses. Property of
every description plundered and destroyed, buildings burned, the surviving inhabitants dispersed,
and driven through the wilderness, to seek subsis-

tence wherever they could find it. This, sir, is a
faint description of Wyoming destruction in 1778.
The savages continued their depredations in a
greater or less degree, until 1782.

"Lest I intrude on your patience, will conclude.

"I am, with respect, your humble servant,

"SAMUEL GORE."

The venerable man received his pension and was
much comforted by it during his surviving years.
He died in 1836. The petition and letter are copied
verbatim.

While the battle was raging, and the women and
children were in the fort for protection, Mrs. Gore,
the anxious mother, was watching at the door of
the fort, to hear the first report that should arrive ;
she was told by one who approached her, that
three of her sons, Ralph, Silas and George, were
slain ; and that John Murphy and Timothy Pierce,
her two sons-in-law, were lying by them all
scalped, tomahawked, and mangled corpses ! Who
can conceive the agony of this mother as she exclaimed, "Have I *one* son left ?" She died many
years ago, and a monument has recently been set
over her grave, together with that of her son, Obadiah Gore, and his wife, by their grandchildren
and great-grandchildren.

The next day after the battle, when the fort was
pillaged, all the feather-beds that could be found,
the labor of many a careful mother and daughter,
were carried out near the bank of the river, and
there opened, and for the merriment of the savages, and the feathers scattered to the winds.

They went to Mr. Gore's house, built a fire in the hall, and stood by it until it was enveloped in flames, and the distressed family dared not whisper an objection. The feathers of the " Wyoming Bed" were gathered up by the children of the family, placed in the first case they could find, and secreted while the Indians were sacking the fort.

There was great wailing as one after another came in, bringing appalling reports from the battle-field, while the savages were entertaining themselves by a general conflagration of the buildings in the settlement, and the despairing inhabitants were fleeing.

In their terror, dismay and haste, the family procured a horse, threw this bed across it, and started for the Delaware, seventy miles through the wilderness, called the "Shades of Death." The old people and the little ones rode alternately, and thus they pressed on their way, in hushed silence. One of the children hurt her unprotected feet, and cried aloud. From terrible necessity, the heavy-hearted mother said, "Stop crying, child, the Indians will be after us." The little girl was quiet, and trudged along without complaining. There were scenes of suffering among the fugitives all the way, such as cannot be described. Hunger, sickness, and death, were common.

An infant child of Mrs. Fish died on the way. The mother could not bury it in the wilderness lest the wolves might devour it. She therefore carried it in her arms twenty miles to a German settlement, where it was buried.

An aged lady of 85, who has just died, said she

was born in Mr. Stroud's barn, on the way to Delaware, just after the massacre, and there were many such cases.

The Wyoming Bed was ever an object of great interest to the children, and often, while making it, and turning it over, we imagined an Indian inside of it, and springing to the floor, would make rapid flight, with more than fancied terror.

The bed has been preserved, and is still among our treasures. Little Frances Slocum, five years old, was taken from her mother's side, carried into perpetual captivity, and never heard from until she became so accustomed to Indian life, that she preferred it to that of returning to live with her friends, who heard from her, and went to her after a separation of near sixty years, and endeavored to persuade her to return to her friends at Wyoming. But no argnments could prevail with her to go home with them. She preferred to be the Indian Queen of the Miamees. The language seemed to be :

"Let me stay at my home in the beautiful West,
  Where I played when a child: in my age let me rest,
  Where the bright prairies bloom, and the wild waters play,
  In the home of my heart, dearest friend, let me stay."

Her own account of her captivity was, "After the Indians took me to the woods, 'Tack Horse,' dressed my hair in Indian fashion, and painted my face ; he then dressed me up, and put on me beautiful wampum beads, and make me look very fine. They were very kind to me." Thus she was diverted, and as they were passing up the river, in the canoe, to Tioga, where they took their captives ; this little one was allowed to amuse herself by paddling in the water, and when on land to practice with her little bow and arrow, for entertainment. In 1789 Mrs. Slocum made a journey to Tioga Point, hoping to find her child among some prisoners who were to be surrendered—but she found her not.

Frances died in 1847, and had a Christian burial, at the " Deaf Man's Village," near Fort Wayne, Indiana. This touching account is given at length in Mr. Pike's history of Wyoming.

IV

QUEEN ESTHER.

THE history of Queen Esther is one of remark-able interest. She led the Indians into the fort at the time it was surrendered; and presided at the fatal ring, of which Mrs. Durkee, an aged aunt, gives the following account: "Fifteen or sixteen of our men, who had been taken prisoners by the Indians, were assembled to receive their death-blow, by the hand of Queen Esther, a large, middle-aged Seneca squaw, who had such honors assigned her.

"In this case, it was thought to be revenge for the death of her son, who was killed by the whites.

"Some of the prisoners made their escape from the ring; others attempted it, but were unsuccess-ful. Among these, was George Gore, who had broken through the ring, and ran for the river, but was overtaken by an Indian, who, with his knife and tomahawk, cut him to pieces. He was an active and handsome young man. His hat was picked up and taken to his friends at the fort."

The remaining twelve or more were murdered with the tomahawk, by the hand of this savage

Queen, on the "Bloody Rock," which may still be seen.

Queen Esther's residence was near Tioga Point. Her village was of considerable size, two or three miles below the present village of Athens, on the west side of the river, and within the township. It is said it contained about seventy houses, of rude form.

An expedition to Tioga was planned by Colonel Heartly, in September, after the battle, to destroy Indian towns and break up their hiding places.

With a small array of soldiers, they marched on their hazardous way toward Sheshequnnunck, where they took fifteen prisoners, killed and scalped a chief, and the rest fled. They made valuable discoveries, and moved rapidly towards Tioga Point.

Captain Spalding, afterwards known among us as General Spalding, of Sheshequin, had command of the 2nd division. They were told that young Butler, a Tory, with his Royal Greens, had just fled from Tioga with 300 men, toward Chemung, 14 miles off, where they were fortifying, and were 1,000 strong. Colonel Hartley was not prepared to meet them, and after burning Tioga, Queen Esther's town, and palace, and all the Indian settlements in his way, crossing the "Sheshequin Path," he returned to Sunbury, where a vote of thanks was passed for Colonel Hartley and his brave men.

Captain Spalding is spoken of as having been efficient in that enterprise. They accomplished much, and brought speedy retribution upon Queen Esther and her associates, for the untold misery they had inflicted upon Wyoming three months before.

Though savage in time of war, Queen Esther was represented as quiet and trustful in time of peace. After the war closed she was often passing from Tioga to Onondaga, unprotected. One time while Mrs. Durkee was residing in Scipio, N. Y., she came to her house in the evening, on her way to Onondaga, with a sister, who was much intoxicated, carrying a papoose upon her back, and inquired in broken English, if they could stay there through the night and sleep on the kitchen floor; Mrs. D. being well acquainted with her, she was permitted to stay until morning, and then went on her way. It has excited some wonder how this Indian Queen came by her Jewish name. If, as some suppose, the Indians have descended from the lost tribes of Israel, it might thus be accounted for, or what is more probable, she might have derived it from the Moravian Missionaries, who had many stations among them, and whose names they often adopted. She married Tom Hill, an Indian as forbidding as herself, and after she left Tioga she went to Onondaga to reside.

Some writers have identified Catharine Monteur with Queen Esther, of Bloody Rock notoriety; others say this is improbable, and that the general supposition concerning Catharine, is, that she was the daughter of an early French Governor of Canada, taken captive when a child, afterwards becoming the wife of a Seneca Chief, and was a lady

of comparative refinement. Her residence was at
Seneca Lake. The Indian village called Catha
rine's town, named for her, was destroyed by Sullivan's army. She subsequently lived at Niagara.

V.

SULLIVAN'S EXPEDITION IN 1779

THE horrors perpetrated by the Tories and Indians at Wyoming, aroused great indignation in
the American people, and Congress determined to
send a military force into their country, that would
prevent further hostilities from them. General Sullivan was placed in command, with three thousand
five hundred men. His orders from the Commander-in-Chief of the American army were to move
from Wyoming, up the valley, to Tioga Point,
there to be reinforced by General James Clinton,
with near two thousand men. Washington gave
orders, contrary to his usual custom, to treat the
Indians with great severity, as the surest means
to bring them to terms of peace.

They were several days before arriving at their
place of destination, with an array of boats and
packhorses, sufficient for their accommodation.
After crossing the river from Sheshequin to Queen
Esther's flats, they arrived near where her palace
stood, which was destroyed by Colonel Hartley's
detachment the September previous. August 12th
they moved across the Tioga river near the point
of land where the Tioga and Susquehanna rivers

meet. Marching up through what is now called
the Welles farm, they encamped on the narrowest
spot of the peninsula, near the bridge, about 190
yards across, and erected a temporary fort, which
they called Fort Sullivan, for the garrison of 250
men, who were to remain there during the campaign. The fort was in the form of a diamond,
extending from one rise of ground to the other,
north and south, and 'from one river to the other,
east and west, guard houses being at each point.*
Many persons now living remember its location.
Bullets have been found in quantities, and several
cannon balls, one of which was found as late as
1830, within the bounds of the fort, and is among
our curiosities.   Indian pestles, stone hatchets
and arrow points have frequently been found,
which denote where the savages have lived.

They waited several days for General Clinton
and his army, then at Otsego Lake, from whence
they descended the Susquehanna river, with 200
boats, by means of an artificial freshet, caused by
throwing a dam across the outlet of the lake, and
raising the water.   When the dam was removed, it
afforded them water sufficient to transport down
the river, their ordnance, stores and troops.

They arrived at Tioga Point August 22d, and
joined the army of Sullivan, under a salute of
guns, with shouts and great rejoicing.   The two
armies united amounted to more than 5,000 men.

It is interesting to look back ninety years, and
notice what was passing here at that time.   Chief
Justice Marshal states that the whole army of

---

*These pages were written within the bounds of Fort Sullivan.

Washington amounted to about 16,000 men. Behold nearly one-third of them, marshalled on this point of land, between the rivers, preparing to move upon the savage foe, protected by a fort, where a vast quantity of provisions was stored for a large army. Behold near 2,000 packhorses grazing hereabouts, across the river, and 400 barges lying at our shores. Scouts were being sent out over these hills and up these rivers to ascertain the strength of the enemy. Listen to the firing of the Revolutionary muskets, and the formidable artillery echoing from mountain to mountain, to intimidate the enemy lurking about the hills, and hiding in the thicket of the pine plains above. Behold the martial array of the army, the music of the fife and drum, and the "Forward March" of the commander of the Western army. Their scouts had discovered an Indian village up the Tioga about fourteen miles, and the army were in haste to reduce it. They proceeded up the river cautiously, for they knew they were moving upon a powerful foe, led by the detested John Butler and Johnson Tories, and Brandt, the wily Indian Chief.

Colonel Hartley remarks, that "Chemung was the receptacle of all villainous Indians and Tories from the different tribes and States." Their engagement at Chemung was successful. They routed the enemy, destroyed their village, cut down their fruit trees, corn and vegetables, which, by the assistance of their Tory friends, they had in abundance, and laid everything waste. It was supposed that very many of the Indians were slain, and many of them drowned in the river. The first engagement was at Chemung, another at Baldwin, then at the Narrows, where the enemy met with a great defeat. Captain Spalding and Colonel Franklin were in the thickest of the fight, and were both wounded. The army returned to Tioga to report victory. About thirty men fell in the battle. Colonel Hubley took those who were killed in his regiment, six in number, placed them on horses and brought them to this place for interment; and on the Saturday following, the bodies of those brave veterans were interred, with military honors. Parson Rogers, Chaplain, delivered a discourse on the occasion, probably the first Christian burial ever attended at Tioga Point. What a mournful procession must that have been, bearing those gallant dead to their place of burial. Where the precise spot is, who can tell? We are reminded that we are too late with our history, to have many scenes of interest recorded, and they must necessarily be omitted. A generation ago, there were many officers and soldiers living among us, who would gladly have entertained a listener with their thrilling accounts. Peace to the ashes of those men! let them rest unknown and undisturbed.

After some days of preparation, at Fort Sullivan, the army took up their line of march, to pursue the enemy further into the Indian country.

From Tioga Point they moved to the upper end of "Tioga Flats," near the first Narrows and Spanish Hill, where they encamped for the night. The next morning they found a fording place for the artillery, pack horses and cattle, to cross the

Chemung river. As the very narrow path on the north side of the river made it impracticable for them to pass, they crossed to the south side of the river, and after marching about a mile and a half, crossed again, and formed a junction with the Brigades of Generals Poor and Clinton, who had taken their route with much difficulty over the mountain on the north side of the river. Colonel Hubley says in his journal: "The prospect from the summit of this mountain is most beautiful. We had a view of the country at least twenty miles around. The fine, extensive plains, interspersed with streams of water, made the prospect pleasing and elegant."

They pursued the course they had taken before, as far as Newtown (now Elmira), when they turned toward the Genesee country, burning the Indian villages, destroying vast quantities of corn, and laying the country desolate.

They returned by the way of Seneca Lake and "Catharine town," the residence of Catharine Monteur. They killed many of their worn out horses at what is called Horseheads, and arrived at Newtown. Thence they returned to Tioga Point, their place of rendezvous. There they were joyfully saluted by the garrison, had a sumptuous repast prepared by Colonel Shreive, enlivened by the music of the fife and drum. They had driven off the Indians, released many captives, and "Sullivan had strictly executed the severe but necessary orders he had received, to render the country uninhabitable, and had compelled the hostile Indians to remove to a greater distance."

That Tioga Point was a place of importance in those days, is obvious. Here were the headquarters of this great army. Here they concentrated their forces. Here were their fort and supplies, and here they sent back their sick to recruit, and their dead for burial. Here they returned after their success in the Indian country, and here again they dispersed and sailed joyfully down the Susquehanna to Wyoming, and from thence reported at headquarters (Easton), "a successful expedition against the Indians."

One of the Oneida Indians was a faithful guide in this expedition. He was taken prisoner, however, and cruelly put to death.

The time employed in this work of devastation was less than two months, and the number of men slain, and lost by sickness, amounted to only about forty.

VI.

MATTHIAS HOLLENBACK.

MR. Miner supposes Mr. Hollenback to be a native of Virginia. But Mr. Peck, of later day, on the authority of Mr. H.'s family, records his birth at Jonestown, Lancaster county, Pa.

Mr. H. came to Wyoming at an early period of its settlement by Connecticut people, and identified himself with its interests, and was valiant for the defense of the settlers, whose cause he considered just. But after the decision of the Court of Trenton, he yielded to it, and was always a faithful subject of the laws of Pennsylvania. He was well known among the brave and generous, in those days that tried men's souls; a man of the common height, but stout, remarkably active, enterprising and successful in business, and possessing strong powers of mind.

At the close of the Revolutionary war in 1783, Mr. Hollenback was employed by the government to supply the Indians, according to treaty, with articles they might need, such as broaches, beads, blankets and whiskey, and made his first establishment quite into the Indian country, at Newtown, a little below Elmira. John Shepard, my father, was his clerk in 1784. It was there an Indian who became offended with Mr. Hollenback, made an attempt upon his life. He came into the store quite intoxicated, with his long knife concealed under his blanket, while Hollenback was writing at his desk. He drew near to him, and when preparing to make a plunge, young Shepard, who had been watching him, saw his knife, and suspecting his design, and having an ax helve in his hand, came up behind him, and struck the Indian a heavy blow on his arm, when the knife dropped and the assassin made his escape.

Before the country was much settled by white people, Mr. Hollenback established stores in many places along the Susquehanna River. He came to Tioga Point in 1783. He first occupied a small temporary building, connected with the house of Mr. Alexander, on a cross street from the Chemung to the Susquehanna River, on the east side of the main street, just above the Chemung bridge, opposite the ferry, and near where Mr. Samuel Hepburne's store was, on the Susquehanna River. The pine trees were growing quite down into the village, but where these stores stood was cleared ground and meadow. Being near the site of Fort Sullivan, it is supposed that the ground having been more occupied, the low brush had not sprung up. The fort is said to have been built of earth and pine brush.

Mr. Hollenback built his store on the corner of the lot adjoining the public square, about the time the town was laid out, in 1786. Very many re-

member this large, two-story building of hewn
logs, in later days clapboarded, to give it a more
modern appearance.   It was a house and store together.   The store was a long room, on the south
side.   On the north were a parlor, sitting-room
and kitchen.   The upper rooms were pleasant and
airy, and all the rooms had corner fire-places, built
of stone.   This building might furnish material for
a history by itself.   No pen has recorded the num
ber of births, deaths and marriages that have
taken place in that one tenement.   Some of the
elite of our country have dwelt there.   Congress-
men, judges, lawyers, teachers, merchants, farmers and mechanics, have helped successively to
make up the inmates of this antiquated dwelling.

It was here Mr. Hollenback opened his "new
store," with its variety and attractions; dry goods
and groceries for the whites, and beads, broaches
and blankets for the Indians, and rum for both.
Mr. Daniel McDowell was clerk.

The country was greatly accommodated by these
early merchants.   Many choice and useful articles were brought up the river from Philadelphia,
in boats for "Hollenback's store," and so great
was the importance of this establishment, that letters to individuals were addressed to "Hollenback's store," and the town itself was known
more by that name than any other.

The Indians did not all flee before Sullivan's
army.   Many that were feeble or peaceable were
allowed to remain.   It is related that at Catharine,
the army found an aged Indian woman, alone and
destitute.   They built her a cabin, provided wood

and provisions for her, and found her there when they returned.

After the treaty of peace with Great Britain, many of the natives came back to their hunting and fishing ground. It was hard to leave the lands they had inherited from their fathers. In a little time they became insolent and troublesome; and when stimulated by strong drink they were dangerous neighbors. At one time when Mr. H. was in his store, an Indian threw a brand of fire through a broken window on a barrel of gunpowder. With instant thought, young Shepard, who was now clerk at this place, seized the brand, picked off the coals, and brushed off the flashing powder, scattered on the head of the barrel, and thus saved them all from sudden destruction.

Judge Hollenback has often been heard to say, that "brave John Shepard had twice saved his life." They were friends in after life, and always seemed happy to meet and recount early times and adventures.

Mr. Hollenback was not long stationary at one place. It was enough to employ his time, to go from one trading post to another, and leave his business with efficient clerks. But he continued to make improvements at Tioga Point. He dug a well near his large "house and store" which still supplies water, "sparkling and bright." He planted apple trees, some of which now stand, and bear fruit, and are ornaments on that beautiful lot. May the trees and the well long remain! He built a tenant house of logs on the same lot near the south line, which has accommodated many a family. Some have lived in good style in these buildings, with neatly papered rooms, carpeted floors, and handsome drapery. He also built a storehouse on the bank of the Chemung river, which accommodated the merchants generally. From there was heard the boat horn, sounding long and loud, more than half a century ago, announcing the arrival of new goods, which produced greater sensation among the inhabitants than the arrival of cars at the depot at later date. The old storehouse at length became useless, was undermined by the water, and finally was set on fire, and vanished from our sight. The tenant house began to decay, and was torn down, and in 1849 the "Hollenback house and store" was deliberately torn down, and the cellar filled up, being about 63 years since it was built.

John Jacob Astor once proposed a partnership in the fur trade with Mr. Hollenback, but having sufficient business to engage him on the Susquehanna, Mr. H. declined.

After many years they met, and Mr. Astor intimated to Mr. Hollenback that he would take care of his son, if he would send him to him, to which he replied, "I thank you, sir; he can take care of himself." Which proved true in the prosperous life of George M. Hollenback.

In 1793, at the time of the revolution in France, Colonel Hollenback was employed by the Governor of Pennsylvania, the agent of Louis VI., to provide a place of retreat for the royal family of France, at some secluded spot on the Susquehanna. He purchased a tract of land in Luzerne,

now Bradford county, which they called Asylum,
to which place a large number of French families
fled for protection, and where several of their descendants still remain.

VII

NEW SHESHEQUIN.

AT the time of Sullivan's march up the valley of Wyoming, as the army passed through Sheshequin valley, Captain Simon Spalding, who commanded a company, was much pleased with the appearance and location of the place, and resolved to make that his future residence. Captain Spalding was a native of Plainfield, Conn. He was born in 1741, married Ruth Shepard, and removed to Wyoming at an early period of its settlement, and died at Sheshequin, in 1814. He was a large man, of fine personal appearance. He was a captain in the Revolutionary war, and was constituted General in the militia after he removed to Sheshequin. He with his family, and several of his neighbors, removed from Wyoming to Sheshequin, in May 1783. This beautiful valley was at that time covered with Indian grass, five or six feet high, to which these pioneers set fire, which ran through the valley about four miles. General Spalding, with his numerous sons and daughters, sons-in-law and daughters-in-law, occupied the upper part of the valley. The sons were John and Chester. John married Wealthy Gore, daughter of Obadiah

Gore, Esq. Chester married Sarah Tyler, sister of Francis Tyler, of Athens.

The daughters were: Mrs. Joseph Kinney, Mrs. Moses Park, Mrs. William Spalding, mother of the late Robert Spalding, and Mrs. Briggs, well known among us, and Mrs. Kingsbury, wife of Colonel Joseph Kingsbury, known as a prominent surveyor and agent.

These all had large and uncommonly fine looking families.

Other families were added to the number: Mr. Fuller, Mr. Hoyt, Mr. Marshall, Mr. Snyder, and Mr. Shaw, father of the surviving son, now over ninety-four years of age.

These families all had pleasant farms allotted them, extending from the river back to the mountain. They first bought of the Susquehanna Company, under Connecticut title, in which state they enjoyed peace, quietness and prosperity, and were able also to meet the Pennsylvania claim, hard as they might have felt it to be, when it was presented.

They found in this beautiful valley, a variety of nuts and wild fruit, plums and cranberries. In a few short years, their presses began to burst forth with new cider, and their barns with plenty. Their butter and cheese, their pork and beans, Indian bread and honey, were not surpassed in their own native Connecticut.

John Spalding, oldest son of General Spalding, was appointed Colonel of Militia, and was well situated on a fine farm of his own, and one presented to his wife by her father, joining his. Colonel Spalding had an erect and stately figure, was lively in his manner, and proud of his wife and of his children, fourteen in number. Visitors were sometimes amused, when inquiry was made how many children they had. One of them would say, "Harry, Billy, Noah, Dyer, Simon, Sally, Ulysses, Wealthy, George, John, Charley, Zebulon, Avery, and Mary. They all grew up to be fine, stately sons and daughters ; but the mother outlived all but two, Mrs. General Wells and Mr. Zebulon B. Spalding, who reside with us.

Joseph Kinney, Esq., from Killingly, Conn., one of the sons-in-law, was a man of intelligence and reading. Some of his descendants have partaken of his spirit, and have been noted for their literary turn. There have been among them professional men, editors and statesmen.

Mrs. Julia Scott, deceased, daughter of the late George Kinney, Esq., of Sheshequin, wrote much, and published a volume of poems, which showed a refined taste and cultivated mind, and her name has found a place in a volume of American poets. She died at Towanda, in 1842.

Obadiah Gore was born in Norwich, Conn., 1744, and came to Wyoming with the early settlers. He was the eldest son of Obadiah Gore, Esq., who had seven sons engaged in the Revolutionary war, a fact of which Colonel Stone speaks in his history of Wyoming as "The most remarkable in the history of man. That a father and six* sons, including two sons-in-law, should be engaged

---

* Colonel Stone says six, the number was seven.

in the same battle field, is rarely, if ever known. Five corpses of a single family sleeping upon the cold bed of death together the self-same night! What a price did that family pay for liberty!" Obadiah Gore came to Sheshequin in 1783, about the time Captain Spalding removed there, and settled in the lower part of the valley. Obadiah was an officer in Washington's army, and served through the war.* While Westmoreland sent representatives to Hartford, Mr. Gore was sent as assemblyman, and was prominent in public proceedings. He was a man of fine appearance, and dignity of character, and pleasing in his address. He submitted to the decree of Trenton, but was on the committee remonstrating against the repeal of the Confirming act, and after removing to Sheshequin, was appointed Associate Judge for the Court of Luzerne county, and served for many years. He was a man of much taste, and cultivated a great variety of fruit. He also planted the mullberry tree and raised silkworms to some extent. He was at one time a merchant, and opened a store of goods in his house on the hill, where he always lived, at the same time carried on farming quite extensively. There was much in his beautiful situation to comfort his family and attract his friends.

Obadiah Gore had five children and fifty-two grandchildren. He died April, 1820, aged 77 years.

---

* Obadiah Gore was engaged as an officer in General Sullivan's army. He kept a connected journal of the entire campaign, which has been read by some of his grandchildren, and which, it is to be regretted, has been lost.

Avery Gore, his son, married Lucy, daughter of Silas Gore, who fell in the massacre of Wyoming. Mrs. Gore was a rare woman. Her domestic management of a very large family, part of the time consisting of four generations and numerous dependants, was a marvel to all who knew her position, more than fifty years ago. " Rising while it was yet dark and giving meat to her household," she would apportion to her domestics the labors of the day, the spinning, weaving, and the dairy, attending to the butter and the cheese, for which she was noted, and the many supernumaries, attending upon all. These duties done systematically, day after day and year after year, with a quick step and a cheerful face ; the impression was, "Many daughters have done virtuously, but thou excellest them all."

She lived in the same house where she was married until the time of her death. She presided at her own table more than sixty years. When we last called upon her, her sun was declining, and she soon after died, in March, 1867, over 92 years of age. The eldest sister, Mrs. Wilkinson, who died some years ago, was also over 90 years old.

Lucy, quite a little girl, was in Forty Fort at the time of the battle of Wyoming, with her mother and two other children. Her father, Silas Gore, and two of his brothers, were killed. Their names may now be seen on the monument, near the fatal spot. The children of the family remembered when the Indians took possession of the Fort ; and many of their antics impressed their childish minds. They placed the ladies' caps and bonnets upon their own heads, put their side-saddles upon their own ponies and mounted them, riding in ladies' style, much to the merriment of all but the poor sufferers. They remembered how the fugitives waded through the Indian meal and corn and feathers knee deep when they were exiled from the Fort. Mrs. Gore, with a stricken heart, made her way with her three children to a boat, which took her to a place of safety.

Samuel Gore came to Sheshequin with his brother, Obadiah, and owned a farm joining his, which was, at one time, considered very valuable ; but some parts of it, as well as other farms in Sheshequin, have suffered greatly from the floods and back-water from Towanda dam.

Mr. Gore was Justice of the Peace, and had the business of the neighborhood at that time. Among the numerous marriages he was called to perform, was that of old Mrs. Nothrop, about 90, and old Mr. Howder, a few years younger ; in about the year 1830. They lived above the Narrows in Athens, and both took their staves in hand and walked down to Squire Gore's, five or six miles, for the performance of the ceremony. Mr. Gore was fond of pleasantry, and told them it was necessary to have some witnesses for the occasion. He therefore sent to some of the neighbors, whom he invited to attend the wedding.

After the marriage, this unique bride and groom took their staves in hand again and started homeward. It is said that Mrs. Howder lived to be over a hundred years old.

About 1790, Mr. Gore was once coming home

from Owego, where he had been to make some purchases, with his knapsack upon his back. He found the Indians quite numerous and hostile at Tioga Point, and the river very high, and could not cross it that night. For safety, he climbed a tree opposite the island, and secured himself by a strap, where he stayed through the night. Early the next morning he went to the ferry with all possible stillness, where the ferry man took him across the river and he went on his way in safety. A part of Samuel Gore's history has been previously noticed, in order to give his petition to Congress, containing a particular account of the Wyoming massacre, and attending circumstances. We have thought it unnecessary to give any other history of that memorable event.

It was inserted in that part of our record, in order to give those statements in their proper chronological order.

Moses Park, of Stonington, Connecticut, who married a daughter of General Spalding, was a Baptist minister, and preached to a small Baptist church in Sheshequin, of which Joseph Kinney was Deacon. They, with many others, afterward embraced Universalism.

His son, Chester Park, is a licensed local Methodist preacher. His ministrations over these hills and among these valleys have been acceptable and very useful.

Mr. Jabez Fish and family came from Wilkesbarre at a later period and settled at Sheshequin. Mr. and Mrs. Fish had been members of the Rev. Ard. Hoyt's church, of Wilkesbarre, who afterward went on a mission to the Cherokee nation, at Mission Ridge, Georgia. They united with the Congregational Church at Athens in 1812. Mr. Fish died in a few years after, and Mrs. Fish lived long to honor her profession. She was much interested in the missionary cause. Her granddaughter, Mrs. Tracy, has recently gone on a mission to Turkey.

Breakneck, the lower part of Sheshequin, was known by that name at the time Sullivan's army passed through the narrows. Col. Hubley states in his journal : "So high and so narrow was the path at Breakneck Hill, a single false step must inevitably carry one to the bottom, the distance of 180 feet perpendicular ;" and yet, an army of more than 3,000 men with their long train of packhorses, marched through this dangerous pass in safety. They then "entered the charming valley of Sheshequin, made a halt at a most beautiful run, and took a bit of dinner."

It has been said that a squaw fell from the precipice years ago and broke her neck, and it is generally supposed this circumstance gave name to the place, and a face was painted on the rocks, by a rough artist, commemorating the event, which, perhaps is still visible.

Obadiah Gore, son of Avery Gore, has a short and ancient record of a title, of much interest, a duplicate of which is as follows :

INDIAN TITLE.

"Nicolas Tatemy, an Indian Chief, bought of the State or Commonwealth of Pennsylvania, in 1873, a tract of land, 180 1-2 acres, in the center of

Sheshequin, and sold it to John Brotsman, a gentleman of Phi'adelphia. This farm was bought of Mr. B. by Obadiah Gore, grandfather of the present occupant, who gave it to his grandson for his name. The draft of land was called Tudelalamoohong, situated on the East Branch of the Susquehanna river, opposite an Indian settlement called Sheshequinung, lying in Northumberland Co., Pa. Returned to Surveyor's office for John Lukens."

It is pleasant to visit the valley of Sheshequin, where so many of our fathers and grandfathers have lived and died ; where cluster so many pleasant associations, and where we have spent so many of our youthful days. We remember while there seeing the total eclipse of 1806, when the chickens went to roost, the cows went lowing home, and the teacher and scholars ran home in dismay.

We remember the old barn, which has just fallen under the weight of more than four score years, and the additional pressure of a heavy snow, the first frame building in Bradford, then a part of Luzerne Co., built in 1786 ; and also the house of our grandfather, built a little later, and now undergoing extensive repairs. We felt like saying " Woodman, spare that tree," when we heard it was to pass through a revolution ; but have been gratified to find some parts of it remaining unchanged, and we can there see the old tall clock, and the spy-glass which Lieutenant Gore carried in the army of the Revolution, and which children and children's children have been permitted to look through, as a special favor. There have been

many living in Sheshequin remarkable for their
longevity. We could name numbers, who have
lived more than four score years, and several over
ninety.

VIII.

OLD SHESHEQUIN.

THE west side of the river, known as Ulster, was called by the Indians Sheshequinung, and was a place of great importance among them. It was earlier known and settled by them, than the opposite side of the river, now called Sheshequin. It was the termination of the great Sheshequin war path from the West Branch, by Lycoming Creek, thence to Beaver Dam, thence down Sugar Creek to Sheshequin flats.

The Moravians state that the Chief Echgohund resided here. It was a Monsey town, inhabited by that ferocious tribe whose emblem was a wolf. Queen Esther's village was composed of a part of this tribe, and they partook of the same spirit.

After the Indians were driven off, the early white settlers called it Old Sheshequin, and those on the opposite side, called their settlement New Sheshequin. They were settled about the same time, principally by Wyoming people, whose sympathies were strong and lasting.

When the township was surveyed by the Susquehanna Company, they included the two settlements and called the township Ulster, which remained so many years ; but in 1820 the township was divided, the west side was called Ulster, and the east side Sheshequin. So that on the west side of the river the original Sheshequinung, has altogether lost its ancient Indian name.

Among the early white settlers were Captain Simons, Mr. Holcomb, Mr. Tracy, Captain Clark, Captain Cash, Captain Rice, and afterwards Mr. Overton, an Englishman, who purchased of Tracy, and was the father of the Overton family now among us. Mrs. Overton, who came to this country some years after her husband, was a lady of polished manners, and very beautiful.

This was quite a social community, and they lived in much peace and quietness. A Baptist Church was formed here, at an early period, and the sacraments were administered alternately on the east and west sides of the river.

Captain Cash and his wife, Mrs. Overton and Mrs. Rice, died nearly at the same time, of a fever that prevailed throughout the country in 1812. Anna Cash, the eldest daughter of Captain Cash, was left with the entire care of her father's large family, and did herself much honor by her faithful attention to them, until they were otherwise provided for. She afterwards married Colonel Lockwood, who was known here many years. She brought up a large family of her own, and died at her old home in 1865.

IX.

JOHN SHEPARD.

IN his journal, written at Tioga Point, and
dated 1784. Mr. Shepard says : "I was born in
Plainfield, Connecticut, April 17th, 1765. Went
to school in the Academy there, taught by Nathan
Daboll" –the arithmetician and astronomer.

His uncle, Captain Simon Spalding, came from
Wyoming to Connecticut, after the close of the Revolutionary war, to purchase cattle. He says : "I
went home with him, and was then eighteen years
old. We had a long and tedious journey—were
fifteen days before we arrived at Wyoming with
the cattle. I continued there two weeks, then
went up the river with my uncle, and remained
with him at Sheshequin until December 18th,
1784. From thence I engaged as clerk for Weiss
& Holenback, in the Indian country, at Newtown,
now Elmira. It was more than twenty miles from
any white inhabitants.

"I continued there until April, then bought 158
pounds (about $500 dollars' worth) of goods of
Weiss & Holenback, to carry farther into the Indian country. Went first to a place called Tioga

Point to obtain packhorses. The streams were high, so that many times I waded up to my waist, and my man Brown was thrown from his horse, and carried down stream several rods by the swift water. We went back to the store, packed up my goods, and started with them the 23d of April, 1785. I came to a place called Catharine Town. There I continued two days among the Indians, and sold part of my load. I arrived at Canoga on Cayuga lake, the 29th of April." (Canoga is nearly opposite Aurora, and noted as the birthplace of Red Jacket.)

"The 6th of May I sent my man back to Weiss & Holenback's store with skins and furs to exchange for more goods. During his absence I lived nine days without seeing any person except savages. I amused myself by walking about, but dared not go out of sight of my cabin, for fear of having my goods stolen.

"May 15th, Messrs. Leonard and Dean came by way of Seneca river and lake, with a boat load of goods from Albany, and in two days more six boat loads came. I sold to them sundry articles, bought of them gum, flour, brooches, blankets, &c. I went to Newtown the first day of June. The night I arrived there the Indians had a drunken frolic, and fell upon us, and we were obliged to make our escape.

" I went to Canoga again, June 18th, and sent William to Tioga Point. After his return, I was taken sick with fever and ague, which continued until October. I started for Tioga Point, and at Newtown met two men from Niagara, who told me that the Indians had killed and taken a number of white people, and there was much alarm.

"That night I came back to Tioga Point. William stayed with me until the 4th of January, 1786.

"The State line was run this year by Rittenhouse and others. I engaged with Holenback again as clerk at Tioga Point, and continued with him through 1787."

It would seem that the Indians had become quite numerous and troublesome about this time. Many of them had returned with strong attachments to their native soil. Some felt that they had not been fairly dealt with, and many were influenced by the love of strong drink, with which they could here be supplied, and here was their incomparable hunting and fishing ground.

With these attractions, many of the natives were returning, which created serious apprehensions among the white people.

Two intoxicated Indians were at one time in a quarrel. One ran into Holenback's store, the other pursued him with his rifle and shot him dead, then made his escape—the blood streaming in every direction about the store. Mr. Shepard witnessed this terrible scene. They seldom offered him any violence. He was quite a favorite with them. They admired his bravery, sometimes calling him "Yankoo Bravoo," and he often went by the name of "Conidehetcut" among them. He in return admired some of their characteristics, and often expressed much regard for them.

While the natives remained, there was much

trade with them in the article of furs. They
found "plenty bear, plenty deer" on the mountains and plains. The dense pines within the hills
and rivers formed a cool retreat for them, from the
sultry sun in summer, and protection from the cold
blasts of winter.

Deer skins were abundant, and from several
bills among Mr. Shepard's old papers, it appears
that other animals abounded. One bill of sale
mentions—24 bear skins, 31 martin and mink
skins, 5 fishers, 2 otters, 1 wild cat, 44 raccoons.

The journal continues: "January, 1788,
bought Prince Bryant's mills, and an adjoining
lot of Nathaniel Shaw, called the mill lot, on which
were a saw mill, grist mill, and two dwelling
houses." These lots were the first land purchase
made by Mr. Shepard. They were bought under
Connecticut title. Subsequently the Pennsylvania title was demanded and met. This purchase
enbraced the land on both sides of Cayuta or
Shepard's Creek, from the State line down to Morley's mill, including Milltown. It was in the deed
called a gore of land, containing 600 acres, for
which he paid 600 pounds New York currency,
$2.50 per acre.

In this purchase, the grist mill was an important acquisition, being the only one within 50
miles. It was run both night and day. Loads of
grain were brought to it from distances of twenty,
thirty and fifty miles, in boats, canoes, carts and
sleighs.

Mr. Shepard was once returning from New
York in a buggy, and was overtaken by a heavy

snow storm, 150 miles from home, which made it necessary for him to exchange his vehicle for a sleigh. More difference was required than Mr. S. was prepared to advance, but said he, "I will give you my note." The landlord hesitated, as he was an entire stranger. When Mr. S. said, "Have you ever heard of 'Shepard's Mills?'" "O, yes." "I am the man," said Mr. S. "Well," said the landlord, "Take the sleigh and give me your note."

Among Mr. Shepard's papers is a statement of the "Boundaries of a lease dated March, 1787, from the Chiefs of the Senecas and Cayugas, to Benjamin Birdsall, Simon Spalding, John Shepard, Matthias Holenback, Obadiah Gore, Elijah Bush and many others, beginning at the Narrows, five miles above Newtown, on the Tioga; thence east to Awaga Creek; thence down the Awaga to the Susquehanna river; thence down said river until it strikes the Pennsylvania line; then on said line until it strikes the 79 mile stone; from thence, a northerly course to the place of beginning." But little is known respecting this lease, except the above description. The Indians lost their lands, and it is supposed that the "Lease Company" did not receive much emolument from them.

June 3d, 1790, Mr. Shepard married Anna, daughter of Judge Gore, of Sheshequin, and settled on a farm at Milltown, which he bought of John Jenkins under Connecticut title, for the sum of one hundred pounds, Pennsylvania money; containing about three hundred and forty acres on

the opposite side of the creek from the mills. He
lived on this farm more than twenty years. Six
of his children were born there. His wife and eldest son died there. Near the close of the last
century he made large purchases of land, and at
one time owned on the State line, from the Tioga
to the Susquehanna river.

In 1796, he says, "Purchased of T. Thomas, of
Westchester County, 1,000 acres of land in the
State of New York, beginning 52 rods east of 59
mile stone." The consideration for the same was
two thousand pounds lawful money of the United
States. This purchase embraced the whole of
Waverly, Factoryville and several farms back on
the hill.

Some years after this purchase, Mr. Shepard in
terceded with General Thomas, to set off a portion of his large patent, extending to Buckville,
for church purposes, which he consented to do.
But the object was deferred, and the General becoming weary of his vast possessions, having no
children, left all to his wife.

Mr. Shepard built a house for his brother-in-law,
Josiah Pierce, near Chemung river, on the hill.
This was a house of entertainment for travellers,
and accommodated the long train of judges, lawyers and witnesses on horseback that passed
back and forth during the sessions of Court held
alternately at Owego and Newtown, shire towns for
old Tioga County.

Mr. Pierce had a son Chester, 18 years old, who
was riding a spirited horse through the pines,
towards Milltown. When about half way, a boy

frightened the horse, and young Pierce was thrown from the saddle. One of his feet caught in the stirrup, and he was dragged on the ground, and so injured that he very soon died.

He was the first one interred in the Milltown burying ground. The Pierce place was afterwards owned by Isaac Shepard, son of John Shepard, whose extensive grounds are now in the possession of his sons C. H. and W. W. Shepard. The house was burned in 1853.

The journal adds, "December, 1798, my grist-mill was burned, and with hard labor saved the saw-mill. Rebuilt the grist mill, and with the assistance of friends had the mill in operation in about six weeks." Such was the spirit of the people at this period.

During this suspension of the mill, the long canoe was dispatched with grain for Holenback's mills at Wilkesbarre, 80 miles distant, and the horse mill of Mr. Alexander was in operation day and night, to supply the inhabitants with bread.

1799. The Compromising law was passed by the Legislature of Pennsylvania. This was followed by law suits about the improvements on lands that had been occupied by Conneticut claimants.

Colonel Pickering suggested the Compromising law, and was the principal agent in securing its enactment, although he was decidedly in favor of Pennsylvania. In his "Concise Narrative" he admits, " That it is not surprising that Connecticut should claim that part of Pennsylvania which was comprehended in a charter, twenty years older than Mr. Penn's, and that all things considered, the Pennsylvania Legislature should be disposed to view the subject in dispute in the most favorable light for the unfortunate settlers."

By the terms of this law, " Commissioners appointed by the State, were to re-survey lots claimed by the Connecticut settlers, a certificate was to be issued to the State, on presenting which to the land office, and paying the small compensation fixed, he should receive a patent."*

It was a time of prosperity with Mr. Shepard about the beginning of this century. His grist-mill, saw-mill, fulling-mill, oil-mill, and distillery afforded him quite a revenue, although attended with great expense. His zeal in land purchases were almost unbounded. Whenever he heard of land to be disposed of, he would secure it if possible. But taxes, and Pennsylvania claims, began to be so onerous that it checked his ardor, and as he grew older, he felt that in being so desirous for the world he was only pursuing a phantom that had no substance. The providences of God, too, were preparing him to look at life in its true light.

In 1804 his diary says, "Began to build my large house in Milltown this season, and made preparations to build my new mill near the river."

1805. " At this time I began to see there was a God that governs the world. This year he brought heavy afflictions upon me, to which I was not resigned, but hope I may realize in his own time it is for good."

*Miner's History.

Febuary 7th, "My first born son Prentice was taken from me by death, with a very short illness. A fall while skating produced dropsy on the brain, and he died in about six weeks. He was a fine looking youth, 15 years old, large of his age, and the pride of his father."

August. "My uncle, Doct. Amos Prentice, next door, was taken from us by death, with a very short illness." Dr. P. was a much esteemed friend, whose society he prized, and on whom he depended as family physician, and instructor for his children.

September 7th. "The wife of my youth was taken from me by death, by a fall from a carriage. She remained unconscious until the next day." A short time before her death, which occurred 30 hours after receiving her injury, she revived and looking around upon her husband and six children, was only able to say, "I am going to the world of spirits."

"Is it nothing to you, all ye that pass by, behold and see if there be any sorrow like unto my sorrow which is done unto me, wherewith the Lord hath afflicted me in the day of his fierce anger."

1806. In the fall of this year Wm. Prentice, son of Dr. Prentice, a lawyer on whom Mr. Shepard depended to assist him in business, died of fever. With all these afflictions upon him at once, he made arrangements for his family, and still pursued his business, sorely bereaved as he had been. He finished his mill toward the river, and his large house at Milltown.

He purchased his first Pennsylvania title of the

Howel Company, with Philip Cranse, 500 acres on the west side of the river, on the State line. This tract included the farms of Cranse, Dr. Woodwŏrth, Robb, Fordham and Wheelock.

1809. "Sold my old mill to Samuel Naglee of Philadelphia."

June. "Sent to Stonington, Connecticut, for my sister Grant, a widow, to keep house for me." (She brought two daughters with her, afterwards Mrs. Stephens and Mrs. Howard.)

1807. Thomas Shields presented his claim as Pennsylvania landholder, against the farm Mr. Shepard had bought of Jenkins, under Connecticut title, and where he had lived with his family many years, adjoining the Howel and Pickering tract, containing 384 acres, for which he paid Mr. Shields the sum of 1590 dollars in different instalments. In those days we heard much about paying for land twice.

1808. " Josiah Crocker came from Lee, Massachusetts with a large family of Puritanic stamp. He was the first person that held regular religious meetings uniformly on the Sabbath, in Athens, and taught the Assembly's catechism."

1807. "Built saw-mill and fulling mill with Joseph Crocker." This was the mill at Factoryville, which Mr. A. Brooks afterwards bought and enlarged for a woolen manufactory, and was burned in 1853.

1809. Mr. Shepard received his first commission as Justice of the Peace from Governor Simon Snyder, to officiate in the township of Athens and Ulster, County of Lycoming. In 1812 the County of

Bradford was created out of Lycoming County, embracing the northern townships, including Athens, and he received another Commission constituting him a Justice of the Peace in Athens, Bradford County.

May 18th, 1811, Mr. Shepard married his second wife on Long Island, a Miss Hawkins, of Stony Brook, a lady of remarkable equanimity of temper, and very companionable with the children she had adopted.

She had five children, two sons and three daughters. She died January 18th, 1844.

1813. The journal continues, "Sold my house in Milltown to Benjamin Jacobs, with 90 acres of land."

1814, "Made a contract for Pickering tract of 614 acres. In June removed my family on this tract." (Harris place).

Mr. Shepard made great improvements on this farm. He hired four "Green Mountain Boys," who had come to seek a place in the new country, for the purpose of clearing off the dense yellow pine timber. The trees readily fell before these active woodmen. It was quite a source of amusement to the youngsters to stand in the door, or look out of the windows, and see the falling and hear the crashing of the trees as they tumbled to the ground, and then the rolling of the logs together, preparatory to burning. It was interesting at the time of the burning of the fallows, to see the curling smoke and ascending flames, and we can now easily credit the theory since advanced that "artificial rains can be produced by combustion."

Without understanding the theory, we noticed the fact, when we were children, and always looked for a shower in hot weather, soon after the burning of a fallow.

1814. This year there was heavy snow and a hard winter. The wolves were driven down from the mountains in search of food, and many sheep were devoured by them. They could be heard howling at all times of night. The inhabitants were much in fear of them, and were afraid to pass from Milltown to Athens, even in the day time. There was no travelling after dark, so great was the fear and danger. The sheep were often called into the door-yard, and lights were kept burning for their protection. Bears and panthers were sometimes seen between the rivers. Bounties were offered for killing these animals, and those that were not killed retired to the mountains.

1817. "Removed my family from Pickering tract to Campbell farm on Howell tract. Built a house, barn, shed, &c." This was the last of my father's earthly homes. Here he lived 20 years. This we now call "the old place." He still possessed much activity of spirit, and was. engaged in disposing of the lands he had accumulated, upon which the taxes and state claims had become quite burdensome. He managed to retain a comfortable portion for his family, and gave much for benevolent objects, often paying a large share of the minister's salary, and always extended an open hand to the poor, not unfrequently presenting a deed of five acres of land to families that were needy. Even at this late period of life, his alert mind would often suggest improvements and advantages for others. About the year 1820 an article written by a traveller, in the distant regions of California, came to his notice and greatly interested him. The writer described the climate as delightful, and the soil as incomparably rich, and abounding in ores. " Gold was frequently seen glittering in the earth of which the rough wigwams of the Indians were built, they, at that time, not comprehending its value." After this, Mr. Shepard was often heard to say, " If I were a young man I would go to California." He did not go to California, but, in 1849 two grandsons, and a little later, two sons and three other grandsons, went to that attractive country. Isaac Shepard, one of the grandsons, in consequence of failing health, attempted to return home, but died on the " Pacific side," and was buried in the sea.

December 31, 1832. "Gave my sons Isaac and Job a deed for the mill at Factoryville, each half the mill and utensils."

This is about the close of Mr. Shepard's memoranda. He began to grow feeble and the infirmities of age were pressing upon him. He arranged his worldly affairs as far as was possible ; after which he devoted much of his time to religious exercises, private and public. He was often heard to pray for a blessing upon his children, and children's children, to the latest generation. He was a constant attendant upon the house of prayer. The Bible, with Scott's Comments, became almost his entire reading, for the last few years of his life. On the day of his death he rode to the village on horseback, returned home at evening, attended family worship, sang a hymn as was his custom, and retired to rest. About an hour after Mrs. S. entered the room. She spoke to him, but he answered not. His spirit had taken its flight.

"Oh, death where is thy sting, Oh, grave where is thy victory," was a fitting inscription for his tomb. He died May 15th, 1837, aged 73 years.

X.

CLAVERACK.

ON the 22d day of August, 1800, Colonel Benjamin Dorrance, of Kingston, Pa., and John Shepard, of Athens, entered into an arrangement by which they became mutual partners in a large purchase of land of the Susquehanna Company, conveyed to them by former claimants.

This tract, lying south of Ulster, had been surveyed by John Jenkins at an early period, for the Susquehanna Company, and was called the township of Claverack (one of the seventeen townships). It was situated on both sides of the Susquehanna, and embraced what is now called Wysox and Towanda.

At this period the Connecticut title to land was held in very light estimation, and considered only of a nominal value; still it was of some importance, as the state government was disposed to treat Connecticut settlers with consideration, and grant them easier terms in the purchase of lands, in consequence of the great losses they had suffered.

On Mr. Shepard's record of expenses on this property, called "mammoth farm," the first date is

1801. Then follows a long catalogue of various expenditures. Among others, in 1807 is a receipt of George Haines, of $45, for "Surveying the undivided moiety of twelve thousand three hundred acres," and another in 1808 of $36, "for obtaining a patent from the State." A copy of the State survey, sent to him by the Surveyor-General in 1816, is neatly and elegantly executed. It shows much deference to the Susquehanna Company, finding their allotments, and is bounded by the same limits.

The whole amounted to thirteen thousand and six acres, and deducting 826 acres re-leased to owners under Pennsylvania titles, left 12,180 acres.

This mammoth farm added not a little to Mr. Shepard's cares and labors. It cost him many wearisome days and nights, travelling back and forth from his home, and was often attended with perplexities.

The late Col. J. M. Piolette, Esq., acted as attorney for Col. Dorrance many years. Messrs. Piolette and Shepard were often engaged together in business relating to this land, in selling and giving deeds of release, to those who would obtain a patent for themselves. The business was brought to a close about 1830. Numerous settlers located in Claverack, early in the beginning of the this century, more on the east than on the west side of the river. In Wysox, the names of Pierce, Morgan, Coolbaugh, Ridgway, York, Warner, and Price, appear among the early settlers, and the mills of Squire Myres, the elder, gave employment to many, while Holenback's store, near Breakneck road, in the long log building, gave life to the place.

Mansville, or Towanda, on the opposite side of the river, was a solitary street for some years after the opening of the new century, and apparently a place of not much promise. Some of the early settlers were Means, Mix, Fox, Bingham, Tracy, Patten and Hale. A public house, a store, and Mrs. Gregory's school, made attractions, and brought many to the place. The school became quite celebrated, and children were sent from some distance to receive the benefit of Mrs. G.'s instruction and discipline, which was thought severe, but proved beneficial.

Mr. Gregory purchased of Shepard and Dorrance, under the Connecticut title, two valuable lots, Nos. 57 and 58, containing 177 acres, in the north part of Towanda, but was not able to secure a patent from the State. He therefore sold his improvement, and the lots were assigned to Mr. Shepard, who sold them in 1818 for about 60 cts. per acre.

After the division of the lots in the township of Claverack, between the parties, in 1826 Mr. Dorrance leased the most of his lands, and thereby made himself wealthy. Mr. Shepard, more desirous to bring matters to a close, sold as opportunities presented, and often at a great sacrifice. He spent a great part of his life in hard labor, visiting the settlers on the mountains, and elsewhere, selling, re-leasing, and collecting what he could ; and becoming weary by care and age, he settled up his interest in the " mammoth farm " hastily, and much to his disadvantage. The discovery of the Barclay coal mines, near Towanda, in the early part of the century, and the Bradford county seat being established there in 1812, have rendered Towanda a place of importance, containing now more than 3,000 inhabitants, with the prospect of still more rapid growth.*

---

*A gentleman who has lived at Gowanda, a town on the borders of the Cattaragus Reservation, in western New York, has remarked that Gowanda, meaning a *town among the hills by the water side*, is doubtless the same name as Towanda with us, which is situated in a similar manner.

The ancestors of the Indians on the Reservation having once resided on the Susquehanna river, we may suppose they transferred many of their ancient names.

Recent excavations confirm the impression that Towanda was a town of importance among the Aborigines, and it is probable that the meaning of this name also, is a *town among the hills by the water side.*

XI.

THE COLLINS MURDER.

AS Major Abram Snell, who was then 85 years old, was passing one day, I said to him, "I have been wishing to see you, and talk about early times. You were among the first settlers here, I believe." "Bless you, yes," said he; "my father came here when there was but one house in the place, and there were but few white people about. I was the first white child born in the township of Athens."

"Do you remember any thing about the murder of an Indian, and the excitement it occasioned?" "Bless you, yes. There was a white man living here by the name of Collins, who had accumulated considerable property. He was a steady man, but was taken with the fever and ague, and was advised to take whiskey for a remedy. He became intemperate. There was an Indian living with him, as a servant. In one of Collins' drunken spells, he met him at the corner of the old Holenback house, and, in a fit of anger, killed him with an axe. His body was secreted in the cellar, and the few white inhabitants were in terror, through fear of savage revenge. The Indians collected in great numbers. The white people sent for Colonel Franklin, General Spaldıng and Judge Gore. They concluded it was best to send messengers to a Chief, then at Newtown, and lay the whole subject before him. He called a council of war, and many Indians, Squaws, and Pappooses, came with him, dressed in gay colors, with goose and raven feathers, and their faces painted on one side, denoting that they were for peace or war, according to circumstances. They demanded the body of Collins, to torture and burn him, as their only terms of reconciliation. But he had made his escape. The white people proposed to give up all his property to them, and it was not until much more was pledged to them that they would come to any terms. Money and goods, to a large amount, were brought forward, and the white inhabitants were saved from the threatening storm of savage barbarity."

Mr. C. Stephens' account of the murder of the Indian by Collins confirms the statements of Mr. Snell. He thinks it took place about two years previous to the treaty with the Indians. He says at the time of the great excitement about the murder, the rage of the natives knew no bounds. They collected in great numbers, and demanded the body of Collins, but he had made his escape down the river in a canoe, while his friends diverted the attention of the natives, by engaging with them in forming a ring, of some extent, to search for Collins.

There were then but few white inhabitants, ten Indians to one white man. The inhabitants were in the greatest consternation and terror; nothing could exceed their distress, expecting every man, woman and child would be massacred. The wife of Collins gave up her husband's horses and wagon to them, and many others gave them presents of various kinds, and they became pacified. The Indians took the body of the murdered man, and buried him according to their customary forms, in the back part of the the old burying ground at Athens. We have no date of the time when the Collins murder took place, except that of Mr. Stephens. It was doubtless one of the murders alluded to by Colonel Stone, in his account of the treaty. Mr. Stephens says: "I did not attend the treaty, being very young at the time, but remember seeing the Indians pass by my father's, by scores and hundreds, toward the Point. They assembled near the bank of the Susquehanna River, a little below the bridge, in the rear of Dr. Hopkins' house and the Stone Church, on a low plot of ground, which has since been nearly washed away. On their return to Newtown, about forty of them encamped for a few days on my father's premises, near Spanish Hill, three miles north of Athens. Red Jacket was with them. One day two of the Indians became engaged in a quarrel, and a fight ensued. A third sprang for the crank of a grindstone to assist one of them who became involved in the contest. The Chief, hearing the noise, and seeing the tumult, ran to a dinner pot, rubbed his hands on the outside of it, and blackened his face. My mother said to him, ' Why do you do that?' He laughed and replied,

' You'll see,' and ran directly, without speaking a word, to the fight. The moment they saw him all was quiet—there was no more fighting. Red Jacket, after he came in the house, told my mother that his face painted black denoted peace, which they all understood. If he had painted it red, it would be a signal to fight."*

Mr. Stephens recollects that those of the family who attended the treaty entertained the younger ones at home with a description of the war dance, the music of which was performed by a squaw. The instrument was a barrel, with a deer skin stretched across it, on which she kept time with the drum sticks, and a sort of humming sound with her voice, while the others performed the antics.

Captain John Snell, 84 years old, has a distinct recollection of the treaty ; was seven years old at the time, and witnessed much of it. He was en- thusiastic when he spoke of it ; said the Indians and Squaws made a brilliant appearance with their feathers, brooches and blankets, and a variety of silver ornaments. He would go now fifty miles to see such a parade. He states that the Indians had a row of wigwams, on the west side of the Tioga River, near where the Irish shanties now are, just above his father's, and were often troublesome neighbors. Many who came to attend the treaty passed his father's door. It was a treaty of peace, and representatives from the Six Nations came

---

* Many years after this visit from the natives, significant marks and characters, made by the Indians at that time, were to be seen on the trees, near Mr. Stephens' house.

from Niagara to Onondaga, together with all that had been scattered by Sullivan's army. Colonel Pickering was foremost on the part of the whites.

XII.

INDIAN TREATY AT TIOGA POINT.

THE glowing description of the treaty with the Indians at Tioga Point, by Colonel Stone, in his history of Red Jacket, has been kindly furnished by Hon. G. W. Kinney, and is appropriate in this stage of our history :

In the year 1790 the Indian relations in the United States were in a most unhappy condition. A savage war, fierce and bloody, was raging upon the frontier settlements of Pennsylvania and Virginia; and the strong Confederated Indian nations, inhabiting the country of the great lakes, were, to the regions beyond the Mississippi, acting under the advice of the officers of the British Indian department, and encouraged in various ways by the government of Canada, were gathering to the contest with a determination that the Ohio River should form the ultimate boundary between the United States and the Indian Country. All the sympathies of the Senecas, who had never been quite satisfied with the provisions of the treaty of Fort Stanwix, were with their brethren of the West, as also were not a few of their warriors, although Cornplanter, their principal chief, remained

unshaken in his friendship for the United States.
Still the popular feeling among his nation was
rather hostile, threatening in fact open and general
hostilities.   Just at this crisis the Senecas found
fresh cause of exasperation in the murder of two
of their people by some of the white border men
of Pennsylvania.   The effects of this outrage had
well nigh provoked an immediate outbreak.   But
the government of the United States lost not a moment in disavowing the act, and in the adoption of
measures to bring the murderers to punishment,
by the offer of a large reward for their apprehension.   A conference of the Six Nations was also
invited at Tioga Point, at which Colonel Timothy
Pickering, who then resided at Wyoming, was
commissioned to attend on the part of the United
States.   The council fire was kindled on the 16th
of November, and kept burning until the 23d.
Among the nations present, either collectively or
by representation, were the Senecas, Oneidas, Onondagas, Cayugas, a small party of Chippewas, and
also several of the Stockbridge Indians, among
whom was their veteran Captain and faithful
friend of the United States, Hendrick Apamaut.
The Indians were in a high state of excitement
when they arrived, in regard to the outrage, for
which consideration they had been convoked, and
which was deeply felt.   The chiefs who took the
most active part in the proceedings of the Council
were Red Jacket, Farmer's Brother, Little Billy,
Hendrick and Fish Carrier, a very old and distinguished warrior of the Cayugas.   Old Hendrick
made a very eloquent and pathetic address to the

Commissioner, in the shape of an appeal in behalf
of his people, reminding him of their strong and
uniform attachment to the United States during
the war of the Revolution ; of the hardships they
underwent, and the losses they had sustained
during that war, and complaining bitterly of the
neglect with which they had been treated since the
peace, in consequence, as he supposed, of the
small number to which they had been reduced.
In referring to their services in the field, he used
these expressions :   " We fought by your side,
our blood was mingled with yours—and the bones
of our warriors still remain on the field of battle,
as so many momentoes of our attachment to the
United States."*

Cornplanter was not present at this Council.

Red Jacket was present, and was the principal
speaker.

> " A monarch tall, fearless, sinewy and strong,
> With an eye of dark beauty, and of thoughtful brow,
> To whom the forest tribes had bent for years
> The subject knee.   Whose eloquence reached the heart,
> With the rare virtue in his speeches,
> The secret of their mastery.   They were short,
> With motions graceful as a bird in air."
> A pipe in peace—a tomahawk in war."

The efforts of Red Jacket on this occasion
produced a deep effect upon this people.   Still,
by a wise and well adapted speech, Colonel Pickering succeeded in allaying the excitement of the

---

*The Stockbridge Indians suffered very severely in the battle of
White Plains.

Indians, dried their tears, and wiped out the blood that had been shed.

The tribe and nation to which Red Jacket belonged, were powerful allies of the British during the war of the Revolution, and were among our bitterest foes.

An English officer once presented him with a red coat or jacket after that was worn out ; he was presented with another. Hence his name.

No sooner had the important business relating to the outrages been disposed of, than Red Jacket introduced the subject of their lands, and the purchase by Phillips and Gorham. In a set speech to Colonel Pickering he inveighed against the proceedure, and declared that the Indians had been defrauded. It was not, he said, a sale which they had contemplated, or which they had stipulated to make to those gentlemen, but only a lease ; and the consideration, he declared, was to have been ten thousand dollars, together with an annual rent of one thousand dollars, instead of five thousand dollars, and a rent of five hundred, which only had been paid to them. He declared that after the bargain was concluded in Council at Buffalo Creek, the Rev. Mr. Kirkland,* Colonel John Butler,† and Capt. Brant,‡ were designated by the Indians to draw up the papers. The Indians supposed all to have been done correctly until the year following, when they went to Canan-

---

*A gentleman who was at the treaty at Buffalo, and was now with Colonel Pickering.

†The celebrated missionary to the Indians.

‡The invader of Wyoming, then residing at Niagara.

daigua to receive their pay, expecting to receive ten thousand dollars. They were told that
five thousand only was their due. "When we
took the money and shared it, we found we had
but about a dollar apiece. "Mr. Street," said
the Chief, "you very well know that all our lands
came to was but the price of a few hogsheads of
tobacco. Gentlemen who stand by (addressing
the gentlemen in attendance with Colonel Pickering) do not think hard of what has been said.
At the time of the treaty, twenty brooches could
not buy half a loaf of bread. So when we returned home, there was not a single spot of silver about
us. Mr. Phelps did not purchase, but he leased
the land. We opened our ears, and understood
the land was leased. This happened to us, from
our not knowing papers."

This speech of Red Jacket or Sa-go-ye-wat-ha,
is the earliest of his forensic efforts of which there
is any written memorial. It is thought that great
injustice was done him by his interpreter. But a
gentleman* who was familiar with the language,
and who was present at the treaty, asserts that Red
Jacket, during the sittings of the Council, spoke
with extraordinary eloquence and power. Much
depends upon the interpeter in the preservation of
Indian eloquence. If he be a dull prosaic man,
without genius himself, and incapable of apprecia-
ting the glowing thoughts, the burning words and
the brilliant metaphors of his principal, the most
eloquent and stirring passages—evidently such

---

*Thomas Morris, Esq., who has favored the author with the
written reccollections of that Council.

from the kindling effects upon those understanding the language—will fall from the lips of the interpreter as insipid as it is possible to render language, by the process of dilution.

Hence, from the acknowledged genius of Red Jacket, and the known powers of his eloquence upon his auditors, this speech to Colonel Pickering is to be received rather as a poor paraphrase by a bad interpreter, than as the speech of the orator himself.   The following is the best passage it contains.   After recapitulating his own statement of the negotiation with Phelps and Gorham, and asserting the anxiety of his people to appeal to Congress for a redress of their grievances in this transaction, the orator proceeded :

" Now brothers, the Thirteen States, you must open your ears.   You know what has happened respecting our lands.   You told us, from this time the chain of friendship should be brightened. Now brothers, we have begun to brighten the chain, and we will follow the footsteps of our forefathers.   We will take those steps that we may sit easy, and choose when, and how large our seats should be.   The reason we send this message is, that the President, who is over all the thirteen States, may make our seats easy.   We do it that the chain of friendship may be brightened with the Thirteen States, as well as with the British, that we may pass from one to the other unmolested.   We wish to be under the protection of the Thirteen States, as well as of the British."

During the progress of the negotiation with Col. Pickering, at this Council, an episode was introduced of which some account may be excused in this place as an illustration of Indian character and manners. It was this year, 1790, that Robert Morris, of Philadelphia, purchased from the State of Massachusetts the preemption right to that portion of her territory that had not been purchased by Phelps and Gorham, in western New York. For the general management of his concerns, and the negotiations he knew he should be obliged to hold with the Indians, his son Thomas had taken up his residence at Canandaigua, and was cultivating an acquaintance with the Indians. In this he was successful, and soon became popular among them. He was in attendance with Colonel Pickering at Tioga Point, where the Indians determined to adopt him into the Seneca nation, and Red Jacket bestowed upon him the name he himself had borne, previous to his elevation to the dignity of Sachem, "Otetiani," "Always Ready."

The ceremony of conferring upon young Morris his new name occurred during a religious observance, when the whole sixteen hundred Indians present at the treaty united in an offering to the moon, then being at her full. The ceremonies were performed in the evening. It was a clear night, and the moon shone with uncommon brilliancy. The host of Indians, and their Neophyte, were all seated upon the ground in an extended circle, on one side of which a large fire was was kept burning. The aged Cayuga Chieftan, Fish-Carrier, who was held in exalted veneration for his wisdom, and who had been distinguished for his bravery, from his youth up, officiated as the high-priest of the occasion—making a long speech to the luminary, occasionly throwing tobacco into the fire as incense.

On the conclusion of the address, the whole assembly prostrated themselves upon the bosom of their parent Earth, and a grunting sound of approbation was uttered from mouth to mouth, around the entire circle. At a short distance from the fire a post had been planted in the earth, intended to represent the stake of torture, to which captives are bound for execution. After the ceremonies in favor of Madame Luna had been ended, they commenced a war dance around the post, and the spectacle must have been as picturesque as it was animating and wild. The young braves engaged in the dance were naked except the breech-cloth about their loins. They were painted frightfully, their backs being chalked white, with irregular streaks of red, denoting the streaming of blood. Frequently would they cease from dancing while one of their number ran to the fire, snatching thence a blazing stick placed there for that purpose, which he would thrust at the post, as though inflicting torture upon a person.

In the course of the dance they sang their songs, and made the forest ring with their wild screams and shouts, as they boasted of their deeds of war, and told the number of scalps they had respectively taken, or which had been taken by their nation. Those engaged in the dance, as did others also, partook freely of unmixed rum, and by consequence of the natural excitement of the occasion, and the artificial excitement of the liquor, the festival had well nigh turned out a tragedy. It happened that among the dancers was an Oneida warrior, who in striking the post, boasted of the number of scalps taken by his nation during the war of the Revolution. Now the Oneidas, it will be recollected, had sustained the cause of the Colonies in that contest, while the rest of the Iroquois Confederacy had espoused that of the Crown. The boasting of the Oneida warror, therefore, was like striking a spark into a keg of gunpowder. The ire of the Senecas was kindled in an instant, and they in turn boasted of the number of scalps taken by them from the Oneidas in that contest. They moreover taunted the Oneidas as cowards. Quick as lightning, the hands of the latter were upon their weapons, and in turn the knives and tomahawks of the Senecas began to glitter in the moonbeams as they were hastily drawn forth. For an instant it was a scene of anxious and almost breathless suspense, a death struggle seeming inevitable, when the storm was hushed by the interposition of Fish-Carrier, who rushed forward, and striking the post with violence, exclaimed : "You are all a parcel of boys ; when you have all attained my age, and performed the warlike deeds that I have performed, you may boast what you have done ; not till then ! "

Saying which, he threw down the post, put an end to the dance, and caused the assembly to retire.*

---

*Manuscript recollections of Thomas Morris. Mr. Morris was known among the Indians by the name conferred upon him on this occasion. For many years after his marriage, his wife was called by them, " Otetiani Squaw," and his children, " Otetiani pappooses."

This scene in its reality must have been one of absorbing and peculiar interest. An assembly of nearly two thousand inhabitants of the forest, grotesquely dressed in skins, with shining ornaments of silver, and their coarse raven hair falling over their shoulders, and playing wildly in the wind as it swept past, sighing mournfully among the giant branches of the trees above—such a group gathered in a broad circle, in the opening of the wilderness, the starry canopy of heaven glittering above them, the moon casting her silver mantle around their dusky forms, and a large fire blazing in the midst of them, before which they were working their spells and performing their savage rites—must have presented a spectacle of long and vivid remembrance.

There is a difficulty in finding a record of this treaty in the Office of Indian Affairs at Washington. There is said to be no paper on file having reference to such a treaty. But on examination of the printed volumes of " American Archives," allusion is made to it by Colonel Pickering, who states that he had sent his report to General Washington. It is said it was never ratified by the Senate.

The treaty seems to have been left in an unfinished state. The terms of the negotiation are not expressed, and the form of the adoption of Mr. Morris by the Seneca nation is not stated.

But, whatever might have been the intention of the treaty, it decided for the Indian that the land of his fathers was no longer his, and we must suppose that with much heaviness of heart,

he turned from his delightful hunting and fishing
ground, on the Susquehanna and Tioga rivers,
towards the setting sun.

> " And lo! that withered race,
> Were turned from their own home away,
> And to their father's sepulchres returned no more.

Very few Indians were ever seen here after this
event. Many white people who were born here
near the close of the last century never saw a
native.

> " Ended is their ancient reign,
> Their day of savage pride."

But they have left us their mementoes :

> "Their name is on our waters, we may not wash it out."

There were a few aged and infirm ones who
lingered until their recovery, or means were provided for their removal.

A white man had wounded an Indian. The inhabitants did every thing in their power for him.
He lived in a cabin that stood on the lot where
Mr. C. Stephens now lives. Mrs. Mathewson went
with her husband to see the wounded man, and
took things to him for his comfort. The day was
very hot. An Indian was sitting out-side the
door in the burning sun. His uncovered head
shaved, except the scalping tufts. She spoke to
him as she passed and said, "it is very hot."
"Yes," he said, " it is as if the Great Spirit is going to burn the world up."*

---

*In 1866, a traveller passing through Evansville, Indiana, met
with an old Indian who said to him, after some preliminary conversation, " Me Seneca, born at Tioga, where waters Tioga and

The Senecas and Tuscaroras have reservations in Western New York. One of 20 miles in length, and two or three in width near Buffalo. Another farther south near the Pennsylvania line, on the Allegany, forty miles in extent. They are called Upper and Lower Cattaraugus. The most of these Indians have become civilized, and many of them have good farms, well cultivated. They have a government of their own, with a President at the head, and have churches and schools, where they are well instructed. In their churches they have native preachers, and the best of singing.

There is another reservaton still nearer Buffalo, at Tonawanda. One also at Oneida on the Mohawk, and another for the Onondagas south of Syracuse, where they have made similar improvements. There are some Cayugas living with the Senecas.

Missionaries have been laboring among these Indians with great success, very many years. Mr. Wright, who is still living, has been forty years among them. He is now at Cattaraugus. Mr. Bliss has been laboring among them about twenty years.

Cornplanter was favorable to the introduction of Christianity among his people. Red Jacket never was until near the close of his life.

Susquehanna meet. Plenty deer, plenty bear dare. Me six winters when Injun was driv out der home. Me see near 100 winter. Me not member much. Me be like old bald mountain, nothing on top." Putting his hand to his head, implying that his faculties were gone. In reply to the question where he lived, he said, " anywhere," then said on "Seneca Reservation."

XIII.

FRENCH TOWN, OR ASYLUM.

AT the time of the Revolution in France, in 1790-98, and during the reign of terror, when the hand of man was raised against his fellow man, there was no safety for life or property. The King himself fled to another part of his dominion, and many of his subjects escaped to other countries, for shelter from the terrific storm that was upon them.

Hundreds came to our country and sojourned in various parts of it. A large number formed a colony and were directed to the Susquehanna river within the bounds of Pennsylvania.

They crossed over to the west side of the river, and founded a large town which they called Asylum, in the county of Luzerne, named from one of the French embassadors in 1786. The town was laid out in regular order, and designed to accommodate a large number. Houses were principally built of hewn logs, and some of them were very large. It is said that Louis Phillipe, at that time Duke of Orleans, was here for a time incognito. It is well understood that he traveled about in

New Jersey and New York State, and was some time at Canandaigua, and from thence came to Tioga Point, where he remained a little time, and then passed down the Susquehanna river to the French Town. Arrangements were in progress to have the King and Queen make their escape from France and hide themselves in this Asylum. Certain it is that a house was built far back in the woods, and called the Queen's house. But in January (21st,) 1793, Louis XVI. was beheaded, and the next year Marie Antoinette suffered the same fate. It is said by some that their son, the Dauphin, died under the cruel treatment of a Jacobin. Others suppose he was secreted many years, after which he was brought to this country and was engaged in after life as a missionary to the Indians.

The early settlers at Asylum suffered many privations, and to add to their trouble, their servants whom they brought with them deserted them, which left them very helpless, as they were unable to do their own cooking, and were not accustomed even to dress themselves.

The original French settlers nearly all left. After the change in the French Government many of them returned to France; others were scattered through our country, and a few remained in Asylum, some of whose descendants are among our most wealthy and respectable citizens.

Bartholomew La Porte was one of the number of the exiles who remained. His son, Judge La Porte, was born at Asylum, 1798, where he resided the most of his life, cultivating one of the most extensive and valuable farms in the country. He filled many public places of honor and trust. He was chosen to represent this district in the Legislature in 1827—served five years in that capacity, being elected Speaker the last session of his service. He was elected to Congress in 1832, and re-elected in 1834. In 1840 he was commissioned as Associate Judge of this county, which place he occupied until May, 1845, when he was appointed Surveyor-General by Governor Shank—an office which he held six years. He died suddenly in Philadelphia, August 22d, 1862.

General Durell was a prominent man among the exiles. A part of the township of Asylum bears his name.

A French Admiral, one of the exiles, settled at " Dushore " which was named for him. He returned to France after Buonaparte re-called the exiles, and acted as Admiral in the battle of the Nile, where he fell.

The names of La Porte, Homet, Le Fevre, Prevost, DeAutrement, are said to be about the only original names left. The descendants of the French exiles are numerous, and some of them are living with us.

Early in the present century many other French families came to this country and settled near Asylum. Mr. J. M. Piolette settled at Wysox, and purchased a farm now owned by his sons, who have added to it, and are extensive and practical farmers.

Mr. Delpeuch, Mr. Peuch and others, settled near Towanda. Mr. Peironnet and several other

French people came to Silver Lake, soon after the book of Dr. Rose was published, setting forth the beauties of the country, and in common with many others suffered from the imposition that was practiced upon them.

Mr. Wright states that there has been a great change among the Indians who remain on their reservations in Western New York since 1831. Then labor was performed by the women, and it was thought disgraceful for a man to work. Now all this is reversed. The disgrace rests upon the man who refuses to labor. The people have become essentially agricultural in their habits and modes of life, and many of them are quite respectable farmers. Some of them have become comparatively rich by farming, and many of them have become temperate. On the Cattaraugus Reservation they have a Division of the Sons of Temperance of more than a hundred members, and are earnest and spirited in keeping up their meetings. Education was once scouted by the most of them: now it is desired by nearly all, and the New York State district school system is extended over them, and of the ten schools in operation on that reservation, seven are taught by well qualified Indian teachers.

The old Mission Church has about 120 Indian members, and the Baptist and Methodist churches nearly as many more. But there are some who still cling with more or less tenacity to their old Pagan customs.

XIV.

ATHENS TOWNSHIP.

ATHENS, situated near the northern boundary of Pennsylvania, is within the limits of the territory purchased from the Indians by the Susquehanna Company and by the State of Pennsylvania.

Mr. Miner says that, " Wyoming in its more limited signification, is the name given to a valley on the Susquehanna river, about twenty miles in length, and from three to four miles in width, but in its more enlarged sense it was used to designate that part of the valley embraced within the 42d degree of north latitude.

" The valley, to the State line, has been called Wyoming by the Connecticut settlers, but it is now more generally called the Susquehanna valley.

" The seventeen townships, namely Huntington, Salem, Plymouth, Kingston, Newport, Hanover, Wilkesbarre, Pittston, Providence, Exeter, Bedford, Northumberland, Tunkhannock, Braintrim, Springfield, Claverack and Ulster, were occupied by Connecticut claimants, before the decision of the

Court of Trenton, and were, with the addition of
Athens, confined to those claimants by the compromising law of April 4th, 1799, and its several
supplements."

The northern boundary of Ulster was at first left
indefinite, supposing that the contemplated State
line would form the boundary, and that would be
the most northerly township claimed by the Susquehanna Company.   It was therefore called the
17th township, and was expected to extend a little distance above the " mile hill," where it was
supposed the State line would run.   But after the
survey in the winter of 1786, it was found there
was an interval of two or three miles between that
line and the temporary or supposed line, of the
northern boundary of Ulster.   Therefore, when the
township of Athens was surveyed the May following, the northern boundary of Ulster was removed to its present limit, a little below where
the two rivers meet, thus giving room for another
large and beautiful township ; which was called
Athens by the Susquehanna Company, and added
to the other towns.   They were then called the
" Eighteen Townships," and were acknowledged
by the State.

Hence, until 1786 Tioga Point was supposed to
be in the township of Ulster, and letters for this
place were often addressed to Ulster Post Office
many years after.

In a copy of a letter from Mr. Shepard to Mr.
LeRay, written in 1831, he states that, " the old
township of Athens was laid out by John Jenkins,
when the Susquehanna claim was under the juris-

diction of Connecticut, in 1777, and re-surveyed by said Jenkins in 1786.'' This is the only record we have of this first survey.

The creek near the northern boundary of Athens, now called Shepard's Creek, was called by the natives Cayuta Creek. It has its rise in a little lake by that name in Spencer, and runs in a southerly direction about 20 miles, emptying into the Susquehanna a mile below the State line.

Several valuable mill sites are on this stream. Morley's mill, bought by Mr. Shepard of Bryant in 1788. Wheelock's mill, built originally by Mr. Shepard in 1806. Brooks' factory, built by Shepard and Crocker in 1809, and Walker's mill, built in 1806.

The township of Athens was surveyed by John Jenkins in May and June, 1786. He was the principal Surveyor for the Susquehanna Company, and a prominent man among the Connecticut settlers.

His field book says, " Began May 7th, 1786, first to take the course of Tioga Creek, at the mouth, and run up to a bend in the creek, to a flat piece of land with buttonwood timber, to the north line of the town.* The next day, May 8th, began to take the course of the Great River, from

---

*This river was called by Mr. Jenkins Tioga River or Tioga Creek. Some years after a horn of large dimensions was found by a Mr. Baker near the Upper Narrows, said to have measured nine feet in length. The Indians also had pieces of a very large horn, which they said their ancestors had found in the river, and they, therefore, gave it the name of Chemung, which signifies Big Horn. The lower part of the river is more generally called Chemung, while the upper part, near the Cowansky, is called Tioga.

the Point up to the lower end of the Cove; then
to the lower end of an Island (now Williston's
Island); then to the mouth of a creek six rods
wide, (Shepard's Creek); then to a small creek
where a cove makes up to the shore.

"The distance from Tioga river to Susquehanna
river, 3 3-4 miles.   Monday, June 14th, 1786, surveyed township; beginning on the Tioga north, and
running 5 1-2 miles south; thence E. five miles;
thence N. five and a half miles to the northern
boundary; then on the State line five miles west."

The course of the roads through the town were
laid out much as they are now—those on the rivers following the Indian paths.   The course of the
road through the Point ran near the center of the
town, to a gate.   Below the gate was a street, and
lots laid out of about ten acres each.

The map from which these statements are taken
is interesting to the antiquarian, and is in possession of Mr. Z. F. Walker. It was copied by Major
Flower many years ago from a field book signed
"John Jenkins."

On the margin of the map is a long list of
names of men who were living at the time of the
survey, and stood ready to "draw" their lots.
None but the most aged among us can recognize
more than a half dozen names with which they
are familiar.   Mr. C. Stephens, now 84 years of
age, recollects nearly all of them.

Athens township was re-surveyed by the State
the same year, recognizing the boundaries of the
Susquehanna Company.

That part of the township on the west side of

Tioga river was laid out in farms of one hundred acres each.

The most familiar names of the early purchasers, beginning at the south line of the town, are Daniel McDowell, Nathan Dennison, Mathias Holenback, John Franklin, Wright Loomis, Daniel Satterlee, Nathan Cary (who sold to Dr. Stephen Hopkins) C. Hubbard (sold to Elisha Satterlee and Jacob Snell). Mr. Murray and Mr. Spalding purchased south of Dr. Hopkins.

Lots were laid out much the same on the east side of the Susquehanna, and the names of Benedict Satterlee, John Franklin, Elisha Satterlee, Elisha Matthewson, Slocum, Baldwin, and Jenkins, are also among the familiar names. Robert Spalding owned the farm now in possession of John Thompson.

The building lots in the village above the gate were laid out with much regularity.

It is seldom we meet with a more delightful location for a village than this. The first settlers evidently thought so, and laid it out in anticipation of its becoming a large town.

Two beautiful rivers, the Tioga and Susquehanna, perpetually flow on each side of a valuable point of land, between converging ranges of mountains, and after mingling their waters, roll down the extended valley together. The dwellers of this valley may say :

" There is not in the wide world a valley more sweet
Than this vale in whose bosom the bright waters meet."

The valley through its entire length has ever been considered a beautiful portion of country, and the historic interest is unparalleled. It was here that the refugees from Wyoming found a comparative resting place.

Many families, bound together by kindred ties, early associations, and the most severe sufferings, located in the upper part of the valley, and within the embrace of the Tioga and Susquehanna rivers, which formed as it were protection for these exiles, who were principally Connecticut people, and were thus united by a common sympathy.

The protracted civil wars among the early settlers, the Indian massacre of Wyoming, and the military movements over these hills and through this valley, the soil of which has been made sacred by the blood of our ancestors, will continue to furnish themes for the poet, the artist and historian. A lady on board a steamboat on Seneca Lake, who heard the other passengers expressing their admiration of the delightful scenery, remarked : '' It is nothing to be compared with the scenery on the Susquehanna river.'' She had just come from Wyoming, and testified to what she had seen.

A gentleman once visiting a clerical friend here was so charmed with the scenery as he entered the village that he exclaimed on meeting him : '' Why, I should think you might preach in poetry here !''

The views from some of the neighboring hills are beautiful, and are always attractive to the artist. Prospect Hill, overlooking Gen. Wells' farm, has often been a place of resort for the youthful and vigorous.

Spanish Hill, in the northwest part of the town,

is among the ancient curiosities of the country. It stands completely isolated near the west bank of the Chemung, the State line crossing near its northern point, leaving the principal portion of the hill within the bounds of Athens township. It is about a mile in circumference. It is about 200 feet high, easy of access, and from its summit is a charming view of a beautiful landscape many miles in extent. It is surrounded by mountains, near the base of which flow the Tioga and Susquehanna. Remains of ancient fortifications around the summit of the hill have been seen by many of the present generation. Specimens of Spanish coin, it is said, have been found there. These two facts have given rise to various conjectures. One has given it the name, the other the character of having once been a warlike place of defence. But when and by whom must ever remain a mystery.*

Some of the early settlers who were on the ground before the natives left the country, have been heard to say that the Indians called it Spanish Hill, implying that Spaniards had been there, and the name has been perpetuated. They seldom went on the hill, from some superstitious fear or dread.

They had a tradition that a Cayuga Chief once went to the top of the hill and the Manitou or Great Spirit took him by the hair of the head

*Judge Avery, whose opinion is entitled to much weight maintains that this, and similar mounds in New York State, that have on their summits the appearance of fortifications, are of Iroquois construction, for a defence against the Susquehannocks, their formidable foe, whom they finally exterminated.

and whirled him away to regions unknown.   It
was supposed that he was murdered by the Buccaneers.

It is, however, a good theme for legends, and
several writers skilled in legandary lore, have entertained us with their conjectures.   Mr. N. P.
Willis with his bride visited this hill many years
ago, and also gave his musings to the public.

It has also been said that when the Spanish
Buccaneers were driven out of Florida, they were
never heard from after they left Chesapeake Bay.
There is, also, an Indian tradition related by Mr.
Alpheus Harris, whose farm covered Spanish Hill,
that these Spanish Refugees were met by the Indians near this eminence, and driven to the top of
the hill, where they defended themselves for days
and months, by throwing up breastworks, enclos-
ing many acres, but finally perished by starvation.   Many now living remember the beautiful
flat lawn of several acres on the top of the hill,
and an enclosure of earth 7 or 8 feet high, which
has within a quarter of a century been leveled by
the plow and harrow.

Other legends carry the romance still farther,
and affirm that the Spanish invaders were rescued
from death by the sacrifice of a Spanish daughter,
" the precious price of Spanish ransom," to a
Cayuga Chieftain, who kindly guided them to
" the prairies of the distant West."

It is well understood that there was an Indian
burying ground on the north end of the hill, and
some remains are still visible.

Professed fortune tellers have walked about this

eminence with their incantations, as if to gather inspiration from it. One affirmed that the fabled treasures of Captain Kidd were buried there, and it is reported that some credulous men have during the night dug for them, with the usual success.

The prospect from this hill is delightful. Not wild or sublime, but picturesque and beautiful.

The native forest trees in this region were in great variety. Those covering the pine plains were a singular brotherhood. The old dry trees, killed by the worm in 1796, so tall that they were often used by sentinels in war time to ascertain the position of the enemy, and the smaller ones so dense that it was difficult for the deer with his antlers to escape in the chase. In these pines herded much game which had been the living of the red man, and was subsequently the sport and sustenance of the white man.

There is in our possession an ancient map of Tioga Point, by whom drawn it is not known. The survey was made in 1785, with only the rivers and temporary State line for boundaries.

On this map are laid down the warrants of Josiah Lockhart, Nicholas Kiester, Arthur Erwin, Joseph Erwin, Timothy Pickering, Samuel Hodgson, Duncan Ingraham, and Tench Cox, with the date of their warrants and surveys, and number of acres allotted them. These were the first State claimants on Tioga Point. Lockhart sold to Carrol, Erwin to Mr. Duffee, Pickering to John Shepard, in 1813. The borough of Athens was incorporated March 29th, 1831. David Paine, Esq., was elected first Burgess.

The first newspaper published in Athens was the " Athens Scribe," by O. N. Worden, in 1841-'42 and '43. The " Athenian " was edited by C. T. Huston in 1854. The " Athens Gazette " by M. M. Pomeroy in 1855-'56, (now proprietor of the " La Crosse Democrat.") "Athens Republican." " Athens Democrat," published in 1867. "Weekly News," 1868.

XV.

BOUNDARIES.

IN 1786 Andrew Elliott, on the part of Pensylvania, and James Clinton and Simeon Dewit, on the part of the State of New York, were appointed Commissioners to ascertain, run out and mark the boundary line between the two States, beginning at the point ascertained and fixed by Rittenhouse and Holland, the former Commissioners, on a small island in a branch of the Delaware river. This duty these Commissioners performed in the year 1786 and 1787, by running a line due west from the point before mentioned, to the shore of Lake Erie, a distance of 259 miles, 88 perches.

" In 1784 a large tract of land was purchased by the Commonwealth of Pennsylvania of the Indians at Fort Stanwix.

The land office was opened for the sale of these lands on the first day of May, 1785. The law required that all applications filed within ten days after the sale should have priority of location.

When No. 1 was drawn from one wheel, the name of the applicant, Josiah Lockhart, of Lancaster, with the number of acres applied for, was drawn from another wheel. His warrant was therefore number one, and entitled him to the first choice of locating his warrant.

He located his warrant on the point of land extending from the confluence of the Susquehanna and Tioga Rivers to a line a little above the Mile Hill, from river to river, containing 1038 acres, 94 perches, called Ta-ya-o-gah by the natives, meaning "at the forks," or "meeting of the waters, known as Tioga Point," by the white man ; the gateway or entrance into the State of Pennsylvania for the red man. According to statements of the Surveyor-General, Mr. Lockhart's land must have cost him 26 cents per acre.

This tract was purchased of Lockhart for two dollars and fifty cents per acre, early in this century, by Mr. Charles Carrol, of Carrolton, near Baltimore ; one of the signers of the Declaration of Independence, and one of the latest survivors of that distinguished body, being ninety-five years of age when he died.

Mr. Caton, a son-in-law of Mr. Carroll, came into possession of this tract. He settled with the Connecticut claimants, in most cases to their satisfaction, while with others he had some litigation.

Mr. James Pumpelly, of Owego, surveyed this tract for Mr. Carrol in 1802, and gave it as his opinion that the pine plains were worthless for cultivation, and others entertained the same opinion. But fertilizers and tillage have developed the qualities of the soil, and many parts of these pine plains are now sold for more than a hundred dollars an acre, and some think this a low estimate. Tar and charcoal were formerly manufactured from these pines in considerable quantities.

The territory which comes within our notice has been included successively in the counties of Berks and Northumberland.

On the 25th of September, 1786, Luzerne County was formed out of a part of Northumberland, the northern boundary of which was the State line. The county received its name from Count Luzerne, minister from France to our newly formed government.

On the 13th of April, 1725, Lycoming County was established out of Northumberland, bounded north by State line, and east partly by Luzerne.

On the 21st of February, 1810, Ontario County was erected out of parts of Luzerne and Lycoming. Its northeastern corner was the 40th mile stone on the State line, and its northwestern corner the 80th mile stone.

On the 24th of March, 1812, the name of Ontario was changed to Bradford, in honor of Mr. Bradford, who came from England in 1762, and who was the first printer in Philadelphia, which county was then organized for judicial purposes, and with Susquehanna, Tioga and Wayne, constituted the 11th Judicial District.

XVI.

DISTINGUISHED CHARACTERS.

MANY in this town still remember Col. John Franklin, a tall patriarchal looking man, bent with years and the cares and labors of early life, of a depressed though expressive countenance; his face pitted with small pox, rather negligent of his personal appearance, though always the gentleman, and always commanding the respect and attention of those who knew him. He frequently wore a long blue cloak, and on public occasions a three cornered hat and small clothes, and always carried a little cane, used particularly on funeral occasions, to preserve order in the procession, of which he was Marshal in those days. Sometimes he visited the schools, giving a word of advice, and always presiding at the town meetings.

Connecticut claims, says Mr. Miner, was the object he had pursued with zeal and delight for more than thirty years; yet he would recommend obedience to the laws of the land, although he had found himself disappointed and beaten.

He was called the "Hero of Wyoming," and was prominent in the early history of this valley.

After having labored many years in vain to establish a cause which he considered just, he finally settled in this most northerly town in his loved valley of Wyoming, in 1788, and here lived many years on the east side of the Susquehanna, in a retired and quiet way, and died March 1st, 1834, at the advanced age of 82 years.

Col. Franklin's farm was sold to Major Zephon Flower, and the avails divided between his children. It now belongs to his grandson, Z. F. Walker.

The only complete record we have of the early life of Col. Franklin is to be found in Mr. Miner's book. In preparing his history if he could have had the use of his manuscripts at the commencement of his work, it would have saved him a year's labor.

He states that John Franklin was a native of Litchfield County, Conn. He was that boy who was called to an account, by his austere father, for gazing about at the place of worship in time of divine service, counting the rafters, etc., instead of attending to the sermon. "Father," said he, "can you repeat the sermon?" "Sermon, no. I had as much as I could do to watch your inattention." "If I will tell you all the minister said you wont whip me?" "No, John, no, but that is impossible." Young Franklin named the text, and went through every head of the discourse, with surprising accuracy. "Now father," said he, "I can tell you exactly how many beams and rafters there are."

The touching account of his tenderness and care

of his three little ones, after the death of his wife, at the time of Wyoming trials, is almost unparalleled. Having no person to take care of them, he determined to place them in charge of his kind friends in Canaan, Conn. Harnessing a horse to a little cart, he placed in it the three children, tied a cow by the horns, to follow, and drove on, having a cup, in which, as occasion required, he milked, and fed the babe. Thus he traveled the rough way, more than two hundred miles, in safety, exhibiting all the patience and tenderness of a mother.

He had three children, Kezia, William and Amos. Kezia married Dr. Beebe, a physician of some eminence. They lived and died at Geneva some years since. Mrs. Beebe was an interesting lady, and frequently visited this place while her father was living, and after his death took her father's valuable papers and portrait home with her.

From his first removal to Wyoming, John Franklin was devoted to the cause of Connecticut claimants. Ever active, and ever zealous for their rights, he was prominent in their public assemblies, and wielded great influence.

This made him a mark for his adversaries. He felt confident of the justice and final success of his party, and was unremitting in his efforts in its behalf. He strongly disapproved of the decision of the Pennsylvania Legislature when they erected the county of Luzerne, and proposed him for a representative. He spurned the nomination, and set about founding an *Independent State Government.*

So determined was he to maintain his purpose that Col. Pickering, who had now become strongly interested for Pennsylvania, foreseeing his plans, obtained a writ to arrest him on charge of high treason, October, 1787. He was suddenly seized, and with much difficulty was mounted on a horse by four men ; and while Col. Pickering held a pistol to his breast, his servant tied his legs under the horse, one taking his bridle, another following behind, and one riding each side, they were soon out of the reach of his friends. Thus subdued by six men, he was hurried with painful speed to the jail at Philadelphia.

All Wyoming was in commotion on hearing of the abduction of Franklin, and the part Col. Pickering had taken.

Immediate measures were adopted by the partisans of the Yankee leaders to seize Col. Pickering and carry him off as a hostage for the safety of Franklin. Under the lead of Swift and Satterlee, the "Tioga Boys," or "Wild Yankees" surrounded his house, but did not find him there. He had gone to Philadelphia to inform the executive council of the state of things at Wyoming, and remained there until January.

On the 11th of June following, while asleep in his bed, he was aroused by a violent opening of his door. The intruders were men, twelve or fourteen in number, painted black and armed, come to execute the long threatened attack.

After dressing, they pinioned him, tying his arms together and led him off through Wilkesbarre in perfect silence, and proceeded up the river to

Pittston. They then said "If you will write a line to the executive committee and intercede for Franklin, we will release you."

He refused, and they went on to Lackawanna. They traveled thirty miles before they stopped to eat. They then learned that the militia were in pursuit of them. This hastened their speed. They retired to the woods and remained there a week, and frequently inquired of the Colonel if he wished to be set at liberty, and if he would intercede for Franklin.

They also compelled him to wear a chain because Franklin was in irons in Philadelphia. He carried it ten days, and when they relieved him they inquired again if he would intercede for Franklin. He replied, "I will answer no question until I am set at liberty." He finally agreed to write a petition for "The Boys," praying for their pardon.

They arrived at Tunkhannock and told the Colonel he was at liberty, at the same time renewing their request that he would intercede for Franklin. This he peremptorily refused to do. Col. Pickering returned to his family, having been absent about a month. He had not suffered in health, having had plenty of wintergreen tea, coffee made of scorched Indian meal, and plenty of venison, and some bread. Col. Pickering was quite an epicure. It is said that after this, during Washington's administration, when negotiating a treaty with the Indians, a vast table being surrounded by Commissioners, Contractors and Indian braves, the conversation turned upon the characteristic designation of the Chiefs. One was that of the Eagle ; another of the Tortoise, etc. An old warrior seeing Col. Pickering disposing of his eleventh cup of coffee, exclaimed "He Wolf Tribe." This incident doubtless occurred at Tioga Point, at the great treaty in 1790. After serving his country in the capacities of Postmaster General, and Secretary of State, he removed to Massachusetts, his native State, which he afterwards represented in the United States Senate. He died 1829, aged 84 years. Not a man in the nation stood higher.

Col. Franklin remained a prisoner in Philadelphia jail many months. His health began to fail, and the iron will and iron frame of this Hero of Wyoming began to give away. He petitioned the Supreme Court that he might be liberated on finding bail. The lion being tamed, the purpose of a new and independent government being abandoned, Colonel Franklin was liberated.

His second wife was a Mrs. Bidlack, whose husband had fallen in battle.

Her daughter, Sarah, married Mr. Samuel Ovenshire, the father of the Ovenshire family among us. Col. Franklin and his wife were both buried on the farm he owned, opposite our village.

He was a representative in the Pennsylvania Legislature from Luzerne, and afterwards from Lycoming ; was also High Sheriff for Luzerne Co. He had in his possession several large books— records of the Susquehanna Co., which, it is to be regretted, have been scattered.

The following leaf from the portfolio of an artist,* may be of interest in connection with the above sketch of Col. Franklin :

"Pennsylvania, generally, is attractive to an artist. My object in visiting the State was to study nature in her secret haunts. And no place in this fair creation offers more allurements than are to be found on the banks of the Susquehanna River.

"In Athens, a northern town of Pennsylvania, I formed an acquaintace with the family of an old Revolutionary veteran, Col. Franklin, who had signalized himself in the Revolutionary wars, and had prepared for publication a history of the eventful struggle, so far as related to the vicinity of Wyoming. He was then suffering from paralysis, accompanied with frequent turns of mental aberration. His family were under the apprehension that he was fast passing away, and being desirous to preserve some memento of him, solicited me to attempt his portrait. I was told that I must expect to obtain it with much difficulty and patience, owing to the melancholy prostration of his mental and physical powers. I repaired to the Colonel's house, professionally equipped with every thing necessary for the accomplishment of my design. I was cordially received and conducted to the door of his apartment, and here commenced one of the most extraordinary scenes I ever experienced. I heard frequent cries of 'murder.' On entering the room, the most promi-

---

*The late S. A. Mount.

nent object that appeared, was the hoary headed
veteran stretched upon his couch, with both his
hands elevated, and his eyes keenly fixed upon
me. At his feet sat an old companion in arms,
named Moore (his nurse), who only could control
the Colonel. I advanced coolly as possible to the
middle of the room and placed my easel upon the
floor, when the invalid again commenced his cries of
'murder! murder!! Moore, Moore!' Upon which
the following dialogue commenced : 'Hallo Colonel, what's the matter?' 'Don't that fellow mean
to kill me?' 'No, no, Colonel, he won't touch
you.' 'You lie, he means to murder me.' 'I tell
you he don't, Colonel.' 'Who is he Moore, a
doctor?' To humor his vagaries Moore told him
I was. 'Come this way doctor, I want to speak
to you.' 'Moore don't let him kill me.' 'Nonsense, nonsense, Colonel.' 'Doctor am I dying?'
'No, no, Colonel, let me feel your pulse,' I added.
'Have you been sent here to kill me, doctor?' 'No
Colonel, I have come to paint your portrait.'
'Then do you mean to kill me doctor?' 'Con-
found your nonsense, you old coward,' interrupted
Moore, 'what do you suppose he wants to kill you
for, he has come to paint your portrait.' 'Don't
murder me doctor, don't murder me.' Moore took
hold of the Colonel's throat, affecting to choke
him, while the Colonel with his long arms, pounded Moore's head, at the same time exclaiming
'Moore is killing me, Moore is killing me; take him
off doctor!' I was about interfering in favor of the
Colonel, when Moore turned partly 'round and
whispered to me to be silent, and he would soon

quiet the old man, which to my surprise he accomplished in a few moments. The Colonel became exhausted from this struggle and conceived himself dying. At his request the family were called in to receive his farewell blessing. He was bolstered up and began a pathetic harrangue to his family. The indifference manifested by all present somewhat surprised me at first, but I was soon led to account for it, when the Colonel suddenly starting up in bed, exclaimed vehemently 'Moore, Moore, I'm hungry, I'm hungry! Where is the doctor?' This abrupt termination gave a rather ludicrous effect to the whole scene, and the family, seeing no immediate danger, withdrew, and I approached the Colonel. 'Doctor,' asked he, 'are you a tory?' 'I am not Colonel.' 'What are you then?' 'I am an artist, and with your permission will paint your portrait.' 'Do you hate a tory doctor?' 'I do Colonel.' 'That's right, that's right. Moore, you and the doctor help me up.' We threw a cloak over him and seated him by a small table near the window. Food was brought to him and Moore ministered to his wants.

"It would require the pencil of a Hogarth, or the pen of a Shakespeare to depict adequately the effect which this scene wrought upon me. In silence I regarded the two old veterans, recounting in their second childhood the recollections of the past.

> "'Boasting aloud of scars they proudly wore,
> And grieved to think their day of battle o'er.'

"Thinking I should have no better opportunity

of effecting the object of my visit, I proposed making a sketch of the Colonel, to which he readily assented, seeming pleased at the idea. The table was removed.

"I arranged my light, and fixing my easel, commenced my labors. My subject remained quiet half an hour, when he suddenly threw himself back in his chair, parted the bosom of his shirt and displayed to my gaze a deep wound in his breast. 'Do you see that?' he exclaimed, his countenance beaming with enthusiasm. 'I do Colonel.' 'I received that wound fighting for your liberty, my boy! I want you to paint that in my picture. Yes doctor,' he continued, 'I got it in the glorious cause of my country—the country I love with my heart and soul!' and the old man unable to restrain himself, through weakness, burst into tears. I was affected, so was Moore, who said, 'all he tells you is true, sir.' In a few moments the Colonel resumed his former position, and I continued my task. It was not long before another incident occurred. I observed his countenance grew fiercer and firmer in its expression, until with his mouth partly open, his eyes glared upon me with the look of a demon. Cautiously hitching his chair nearer where I sat, he suddenly gave a kick and my easel and canvass lay prostrate on the floor.

"Alarmed at this sudden demonstration of hostility, I started back, and in so doing raised my maul-stick. The Colonel regarded this movement on my part as a declaration of war, and threw himself in an attitude of defense, exclaiming 'come

on you infernal traitors, you have been trying
long enough to murder me. Stand by me Moore.'
'Pardon me Colonel.' 'I'll never pardon you,
you are an infernal coward, isn't he Moore?' 'No
he is not,' said Moore, 'and if you don't behave
yourself he'll whip you as you deserve.' 'You
lie Moore, I can flog you and the doctor both.'
When a pugilistic encounter began between the
two old soldiers. My picture was not injured, but
I removed to a respectful distance.

"The knowledge I had already gained of the
Colonel's face enabled me to finish the portrait to
the satisfaction of his friends; a sketch of which is
now in my portfolio, which reminds me of the
noble form of the worthy old officer, and his companion Moore. A late visit to the romantic valley
informed me that both of my old friends ' lay like
warriors taking their rest,' on the beautiful banks
of the Susquehanna."

Colonel John Jenkins was a native of Windham
County, Conn.; born 1751 and died in 1829. He
was known extensively through the valley to the
State line, and far into the the Genessee country.
Having been engaged foremost in the surveys of
the Susquehanna Company, he was probably better
acquainted with the country and the inhabitants
than any other man. Every body knew Colonel
Jenkins. During the Revolutionary war he was
captured and taken with others to the British lines.
This afforded him an opportunity to gain much
knowledge in relation to the Indian settlements,
and enabled him to give valuable information to
General Washington, when planning the expedi-

tion under Sullivan. Colonel Jenkins was chief guide for General Sullivan throughout the campaign.

He was a very decided man. He declared he would never yield to the demands of Pennsylvania, and he kept his resolution. He never was conquered, but went down to his grave protesting against Pennsylvania usurpation.

Mr. C. Stephens remembers him well; thinks Colonel Jenkins surveyed all of the seventeen townships, and Athens in addition, before 1786, while the Indians were yet on the ground; that they were afraid of him, and he was not afraid of anything.

XVII.

EARLY INHABITANTS.

TIOGA Point was a place of great note among the Indians. It had been the rallying point for their warriors, and the rendezvous for their traders. Cornplanter, Big Tree, Red Jacket, and many of their noble braves have visited here, and met in council together.

It was at Tioga Point that the great gathering of warriors from Niagara, Onondaga, and throughout the lake country took place, preparatory to their murderous expedition down the Susquehanna, where, " like the wolf on the fold " they surprised the unsuspecting and unprotected inhabitants of Wyoming.

During their wars with the whites of Pennsylvania many a poor heart-broken captive, children ot tender years, men and women, have been urged on their way to this place.

It would seem from several accounts that this was the place of rendezvous for the captives taken in the wars of Pennsylvania. After an unsuccessful battle a man was looking out for a much loved friend ; he was informed that " he was wounded or dead or had gone to Tioga." (Taken captive.)

Soon after the treaty with the Indians, and their removal, further apprehensions from them being at an end, many families of intelligence and means came to reside at Tioga Point, and established themselves in business.

About the period of 1788 the township of Athens or Tiogatown, as it was then called, began to be settled rapidly. Many families came from the lower part of the valley, principally Connecticut people, who had been sufferers together in their various struggles. The heads of these families —Swift, Stephens, Tyler, Mathewson and many others, had bought under the Connecticut title for a small price, and placed their families upon their possessions, where they lived undisturbed many years. But Pennsylvania land holders were numerous, whose claims covered those of the Connecticut settlers, and they were obliged to pay for their lands the second time, according to their estimated value, which, however, was small.

The country throughout this entire Point, from Cayuta Creek to the confluence of the rivers, was covered with pines, with the exception of a few buttonwoods and elms which grew on the banks of the rivers. The soil at that time was poor and unproductive, and with all these obstacles it was sometimes difficult to obtain a livelihood, and the bickerings and strifes about titles were constant sources of contention. Assault and battery were not unfrequent. Murder was many times threatened and several times committed. Mr. Erwin,

the father of James and Arthur, was sitting in his
log house, near where the present McDuffee
house stands, when he was fired upon through
the window and killed.   Ira Stephens, the father
of numerous children, was killed by the heavy
blow of a cudgel while absent from home.   Joseph
Tyler, the father of Francis Tyler, was assaulted
when at work in his field and struck to the ground,
and then beaten till he was supposed to be dead.
He was afterward thrown over the fence among
bushes to be concealed, but he revived and was
restored.   His skull was so injured that he never
fully recovered his faculties.   The family was
broken up and scattered.

Daniel McDuffee came from Ireland to Philadelphia ; from thence to Athens in 1788, where he
bought extensively of Mr. Erwin.   Mr. McDuffee
was a tall and sprightly man, and played well on
the flute.   " Come up to my house " said he to a
young gentleman, who was also a musician, " and
I will show you a raal flute."   He had been a noted weaver in Ireland, and showed his skill in that
line in weaving a piece of linen for a young lady of this neighborhood, which he offered to do
on condition that she would spin the yarn.   The
offer was accepted, and the result was an uncommonly fine piece of cloth, some of which can be
seen at this day.

David Clement and Enoch Paine, brothers, came
from Portland, Maine, in 1794 and '5, and settled
at Athens.   Ancient documents show that David
Paine was employed as Clerk of the Susquehanna
Company, in 1795.   He was early a merchant and

inn keeper, and in 1808 was appointed Justice of
the Peace, and for many years was Postmaster at
Athens. He married Miss Phebe Lindsley, sister
of Mrs. Dr. Hopkins. Both were accomplished
and excellent ladies.

After Mrs. Paine's death he married a cultivated
lady from Portland, who survives him. Mr. Paine
purchased several lots south of the Academy,
where he passed the closing days of his life. His
brother Enoch died there also, many years ago. The
house occupied by his brother Clement was built
by David Paine in 1803, and Mr. Dan. Elwell
was architect. The old hotel was built by Mr.
James Erwin near the close of the last century.

Dr. Stephen Hopkins came from Morristown, N.
J., about the same year with Mr. Paine. He is
said to have built the first frame house on Tioga Point. The north wing of the Backus house
alone remains of it. In 1802 he built his large
house, still standing near the Stone Church,
which he occupied many years. This was in its
prime a showy house, and a place of great resort.
Beside his profession as a physician, he did a
large business as a merchant and inn keeper, as
this was a general thoroughfare. Such establish-
ments were in great demand, and being a profitable
and popular business, many engaged in it. It
was said that his table was not excelled by any in
the western country.

The Doctor owned the farm across the Chemung
River, south of the bridge, which he cultivated.
The high land is still called "Doctor's Hill."

His practice, too, was extensive. Many will

remember his peculiar management of fevers—
that of prescribing hemlock sweats and rye mush.
His theory was that it removed the fever without
debilitating the system.   Mrs. Hopkins was a refined and Christian lady.   They had four daughters
and one son.   Two of the daughters were educated
at Litchfield, Conn., and married W. and E. Herrick, brothers.   One married the late Doctor Huston, a resident of this place for many years; and
the youngest married the late Rev. J. Williamson.
The son married a daughter of John Shepard, Esq.
The Doctor died suddenly, March 24th, 1841.

Joseph Spalding came from Plainfield, Conn., in
about 1796, and settled on the west side of the
Chemung River, with his family.   His son, John
Spalding, has been known among us many years,
and his descendants are numerous.

The Murray and Tozer families came about the
same time.   Colonel Julius Tozer was from New
London, his wife from Colchester, Conn.   Mr. Tozer
and three of his sons were volunteers in the war of
1812.   He had a large family, and many of his
descendants reside in this town.

Jonathan Harris, from Newburg, bought a tract
of land south of Shepard's Creek, near Susquehanna River, under Connecticut title.   Here he lived
many years, but in 1800 a writ of ejectment was
brought against him from a Pennsylvania company of landholders, which required him to seek a
home elsewhere.   He was allowed to remain there
several years.   A part of the farm, where his son
Alpheus lived, on the Chemung River, bordering
on the state line, was bought for him by a son at

Newburg, where he spent the remainder of his days. The farm is now owned by William W. Shepard. The older inhabitants still remember Mr. Harris as a shrewd, eccentric man. The question was once put to him as to the best occupation or calling for a young man. He replied that loaning money was the best business he knew of, but difficult to establish.

Major Zephon Flower came to Sheshequin in 1788, where he remained until early in this century, when he removed to Athens. He learned surveying of Colonel Kingsbury, and followed that as his profession. He bought the farm once owned by Colonel Franklin, where himself and wife were buried. Near them lies Louisa, a maiden daughter, who has often been seen in our streets, with a basket of nuts on her arm, distributing to the children, and giving a word of good advice. When she last called on us, we inquired what she could remember about the famine here in the last century. "It was bad enough," said she, "and a time of great distress among the inhabitants." She said they had a way of cooking up everything that could be eaten. They lived much upon pursley and berries. When the grain was not more than half filled out, they cut much of it, and dried it in their large iron kettle over a slow fire, then put it on the backs of the boys and sent it up to Mr. Shepard's mill to be ground. Sometimes they pounded it, and no one ever ate better shortcake than they had at such times.

Mr. Stephens' account confirms hers, and furthermore says that people began to be in a state of starvation, and showed it in their emaciated looks, feeble walk, and lack of energy. Boat loads of flour were brought up the river to speculate upon. At one time a boat was boarded, and flour demanded at a reasonable price. They had been offered sometimes as many silver dollars for a barrel as they could place on a barrel head. Parents often referred to those times when their children complained of their food. It is thought, however, that none died of hunger. The famine was owing to the fact that a greater number of settlers came into the country than could be supplied with provisions, and fewer boat loads were brought up from lower Wyoming, on account of a scarcity there.

The families of Minier, Morley, Griffin, Green, Lane and Watkins arrived early in the present century.

Joshua R. Giddings was born in the town of Athens. His family were temporary residents on the farm of Mr. D. Loomis, (Queen Esther's Flats,) where Joshua was born. They removed to Ohio when he was an infant. He became a man of reputation, and for many years was a prominent member of Congress. He was distinguished for his anti-slavery principles, which were then far in advance of the times. He visited the place where he was born a short time before his death.

After the opening of the new century many valuable inhabitants came in, which added much to the growth and improvement of the place.

Mr. Stephen Tuthill came here in 1800, and established himself as a merchant in the Holenback

store, and occupied the house.   Mr. Tuthill was a
social, intelligent, business man.   Mrs. Tuthill was
a sensible, noble and Godly woman.   "Her price
was far above rubies."   After some years they removed to Elmira, where they spent the remainder
of their days.   They accummulated wealth, with
which they were liberal and benevolent.

Mr. John Miller, a merchant from Newtown,
built the house now occupied by Mr. Stephens,
which was at that time occupied as a dwelling and
store.

Mr. John Saltmarsh came from Fairfield County,
Conn., in 1801.   He was a graduate of Yale College, and was an intelligent, religious and useful
man.   He built the house which is still known as
the Saltmarsh House.   He often opened it for religious services, when visited by missionaries or
Methodist preachers, before there was any place of
worship there.   He received the appointment of
justice of the peace soon after coming here, and
kept a public house, which was always in good
repute.   Mrs. Saltmarsh was a perfect specimen of
a New England woman.   Mr. Saltmarsh died November 9th, 1815.   His death was a great loss to the
community, and an irreparable loss to his family.
Mrs. Saltmarsh died July 4th, 1847.   They had
two sons and one daughter.   The sons were en-
engaged extensively many years in transporting
mails at the South.   Lorenzo Dow, a man remarkable for his eccentricities, visited this place in about
1810.   He stopped at Squire Saltmarsh's and
preached there.   His preaching was said to be peculiar and very impressive.

The decision of the Court of Trenton in 1782, giving the jurisdiction of the contested lands to Pennsylvania, did not deter the Connecticut settlers from occupying and settling their lands, within the seventeen townships.

This right was understood, from the Confirming act, and other acts of leniency from the State, and it was difficult for the Connecticut settlers to follow up all the complicated laws and changes that the State might make, which were adverse to what they considered their just claims. Hence, they were ever ready to contend for their rights, and all through the close of the last century, and even after the Compromising act was passed, there was constant litigation between Connecticut and Pennsylvania claimants, about land titles and improvements.

Mr. Alpheus Harris bought of S. Swift a valuable farm of four hundred acres, including Spanish Hill, to the State line, under Connecticut title, about the close of the last century. Mr. Harris was a sensible and Godly man. It is said he was the first man that maintained family worship in the township of Athens. He lived on this farm with his family, pleasantly situated, many years, not doubting the validity of his title. In 1810 a suit of ejectment was brought against him by Jesse L. Keene, of Philadelphia, who had obtained a State claim. Mr. Keene surveyed the farm and gained the suit. It devolved upon Mr. Harris to pay the cost, but Mr. Keene offered to pay it, and allowed Mr. Harris to remain on the farm.

Mr. Keene afterward sold it to Pitney Snyder,

son-in-law to Mr. Harris, by whose family it is still owned. There were many cases similar to this. Mr. Harris was engaged with others in the surveying of the State line, 1786-7.

Some favor was shown to Connecticut settlers by applying to the Legislature, although they had not followed the exact letter of the law, and no doubt, in some instances, political power decided for or against them.

Mr. Elisha Mathewson, father of the family well known in Athens, was one of the first purchasers under Connecticut title. He had bought of the Susquehanna Company a number of lots on the flats below the village, passing through the best part of what is now known as the Welles farm, and where the stone house now stands; also a lot in the village, on which he built a large frame house, painted red, in 1795. There Mr. Mathewson died, and his family lived in the house for a long time. The "Mansion House," built on the site of the old red house, is in possession of Mr. Elisha Mathewson, son of the early purchaser.

Mrs. Mathewson being left a widow with a large family, was not willing to yield her claim to her home in the village, or that of her farm on the flats. The representatives of Mr. Carrol, holding a Pennsylvania title, had brought a suit of ejectment in Circuit Court against Mrs. Mathewson, in 1807, in which she failed to make any defense, feeling secure under the Connecticut title. Judgment was rendered against her by default, and the Marshall proceeded to put Mr. Carrol in possession, by his representatives, but was repelled by the family and friends of Mrs. Mathewson, who had barricaded the house, and prepared hot water, guns and ammunition, to quite an amount, for defense.

The Marshall thought best to defer the object for a time, and Mrs. Mathewson remained in possession ever after. Mr. Henry Welles afterwards took possession of the farm on the Point, which he had purchased of Mr. Carrol, and removed his family there in 1823. He built the stone house, barns, etc., and bought out the settlers generally on the farm, excepting Mrs. Mathewson. Her son Constant, having become of age, acted as agent for the family, and pursued his object most assiduously. He repaired to Harrisburg in 1823, and in 1824 laid his case before the House of Representatives, and met with friends who favored his object. In 1827 and 1828 he was chosen Representative and after unremitting perseverance on his part, the Legislature appointed Commissioners to appraise the land in controversy, and paid Mrs. Mathewson, from the public treasury, the sum of ten thousand dollars.

George Welles, Esq., came from Glastenbury, Conn., to Tioga Point, in the year 1799. He was a graduate of Yale College, and it was said of him that "his talents were ten." Soon after coming he re he was appointed justice of the peace, and was engaged as a land agent for Mr. Carrol, of Carrolton.

He purchased many acres on the west side of the village, and built the house where Mr. Harris now lives, and died there in 1813. He was the father of the Welles family, residents of Athens, as also that of Wyalusing. He had three sons and two daughters, all of whom partook of the intelligence and refinement of their noble father and mother.

Henry, his oldest son, was attractive and popular. He early became acquainted at Baltimore with Messrs. Carrol and Caton, who were much interested in him, and through them he obtained the Welles farm. This engaging young man was once coming from Owego on horseback, and as he approached Pike Creek he found a gentleman and lady, strangers, also on horseback, who were in a quandary about what they should do. The creek had overflowed its banks, and it was not possible to ford it. As Mr. Welles drew near they thankfully availed themselves of his offer to guide them through a rough way to a bridge where they could cross. They were greatly accommodated, and as they all possessed uncommon conversational powers, we must suppose they had a social time. They were soon acquinted; Mr. Welles, Dr. Patrick and his sister, a beautiful and accomplished young lady, in intellect scarcely inferior to the gentlemen accompanying her. Doubtless they had an intellectual feast as they pursued their journey down the Susquehanna to Tioga Point, where Mr. Welles resided; and by this time an attachment was formed between Mr. Welles and Miss Patrick, which they had not been anticipating. The doctor and his sister tarried over night to rest, and then went on their way to Kingston, 80 miles down the river, where they resided, with the intimation from Mr. Welles that business might make it necessary for him to visit Kingston shortly. He went, and in a few weeks the lady became his bride.

They immediately started for his home on horseback. They arrived late in the evening of the next day at the ferry, a little below the village, and found it was not safe to cross the river with horses at night, as the water was high.

There was no alternative but to remain at the ferry house, or cross in a small boat and walk home from the river. They did this, and were soon received in the embraces of waiting friends. Seldom has a bride met with so cordial a welcome. Her reputation was known, as a superior girl and a devoted christian. The few religious ladies felt strengthened by such an acquisition to their society. But owing to the dampness of the earth and of the evening air on the night of her arrival she received a chill, from which she did not recover. Her lungs became affected, a cough ensued, and notwithstanding all the efforts of kind friends and physicians, in twenty-one days after their marriage she died, 1809, the early bride of Henry Welles.

After recovering somewhat from the shock of this affliction the business of life again engaged his attention. Perplexities about land titles had already arisen, but having the State claim, he felt sanguine that his cause was just and would be paramount to any other; yet he was much annoyed by the early Connecticut claimants, particularly the Mathewson claim. After much litigation relative to it, the State, after many years, satisfied the Mathewson demand, as before mentioned, and left Mr. Welles unembarrassed, in possession of his princely farm. In 1812 he married again, a daughter of Colonel John Spalding, of Sheshequin.

Mr. H. Welles was first a representative from Lycoming County, and after Bradford County was organized, he was sent two years to Harrisburg as representative, and four years as Senator, between the years 1812 and 1818, from the county of Bradford. Through his influence the Academy Bill was passed in 1813. He became a favorite of Governor Snyder, who appointed him one of his aids, with the rank of general ; hence his title. He wrote to his brother of his appointment, who informed Mrs. Welles that a general would be there to dine. She exerted herself to prepare a table appropriate to her unknown guest, and when the time arrived was gratified to find that the general was none other than her husband. He died suddenly, on his farm, December 1833, aged 53 years, leaving his farm to his sons.

General Welles was seldom equaled in intellectual and conversational powers, and was much admired in society. In his later days he was more inclined to religious reading, and whatever may have been his former views, he expressed his conviction of the excellence of the Christian religion, and his approbation of the benevolent societies of the day. His business capacities were remarkable, and under his personal supervision his grounds brought forth bountifully, and his barns were filled with plenty.

Mr. C. Stephens, the oldest man living among us, was three years of age when his father's family removed from Wyoming to this place, in 1788, two years before the treaty with the Indians.

His recollection of olden times is remarkable, and he has given us much information about past events.

Francis Tyler was an enterprising lad, who finding he must depend upon his own exertions, was industrious and frugal, and engaged in whatever object of pursuit presented itself, and after a few years surprised his friends by purchasing one of the most valuable farms in the country. With his continued industry and good management, together with the ordinary rise of property, he became a wealthy citizen, and has now arrived at an age of more than four score years.

Dr. Thomas Huston came to Athens in 1812, married a daughter of Dr. Hopkins, and took his practice as physician. In 1824 he removed with his family to the west branch of the Susquehanna, and after several years returned to his practice in Athens, where he passed the remainder of his life. He died in June, 1866.

A bachelor, whose name is not recorded, bought of the Susquehanna Company the lot of land below the Mile Hill, containing twenty acres. He had been suffering from hypochondria, and being in destitute circumstances he offered to sell to Mr. Elisha Satterlee his lot of land for a French crown and a bandana handkerchief. The bargain was made, and Mr. Satterlee went home and informed his wife, who objected to the purchase, lamenting that they should have any additional taxes to pay. This lot of land was recently purchased of Judge Herrick by the Railroad Company, for two hundred and fifty dollars per acre.

Edward Herrick, Esq., was married in 1813 to Miss C. Hopkins, daughter of Dr. Hopkins. They made their bridal tour on horse back through the wilds of Pennsylvania, over rough roads, swollen streams, and through an unsettled country, to the interior of Ohio. It required many days to accomplish the journey. He remained there about three years, when he returned in a carriage, with his wife and little son and a faithful negro man for driver. This was Peter Carlisle, whose numerous descendants are now living in the township of Smithfield.

Mr. Herrick was admitted to the bar in Ohio, practiced law in Bradford County several years, and was in 1818 appointed Presiding Judge over the 11th Judicial District, consisting of Susquehanna, Bradford, Tioga, to which were added Potter and McKean Counties. He is still living, at the advanced age of 82 years.

Michael R. Thorp, an agent for the Pennsylvania land holders, bought a beautiful lot on the bank of the Susquehanna, where he erected a dwelling. In a few years his house was sold to Judge Herrick, who has occupied it about half a century.

Hon. Horace Williston was a native of Sheffield, Conn., and the youngest brother of the late Seth Williston, D. D. He studied law with Hon. Vincent Matthews, of Elmira, and entered upon the practice of his profession at Binghamton, N. Y.

He came to reside at Athens in 1819. He was eminent in his profession, and had extensive practice throughout Northern Pennsylvania. As a lawyer he was distinguished for his strict integrity and love of justice. For several years he was Presiding Judge of the Thirteenth Judicial District. Though talented and popular in his profession, his surviving friends love to contemplate his *Christian* character, in the family circle—in the weekly meeting for prayer—at the monthly concert, and in his fidelity as ruling elder in the Church. Young men, just entering upon the practice of the law, have often been referred to Mr. Williston as an example in the profession that would be safe for them to follow. He died August 14th, 1855, saying: "I want to lie down in the grave and rest until the resurrection morn."

These eminent men—Judge Herrick, Judge Williston and Judge Elwell, were all residents of Athens; and Judge Elwell, who is now presiding over the Twenty-sixth Judicial District, is a native of this town.

Hon. Thomas Maxwell was born at Tioga Point, in the Holenback house, 1790. His family removed to Newtown early in the beginning of this century. As he grew up to manhood he was brought into notice by his talents and industry. He was at one time County Clerk for the old County of Tioga, N. Y., and was for many years Postmaster of the village of Elmira. At the age of about thirty he was elected a member of the House of Representatives from the Congressional District where he lived, and his services were satisfactory.

The circumstances of his death were very painful. Passing to his office after dinner, by way of the Railroad bridge, he was run over by a freight train and survived but a short time. The Elmira paper remarked : "The community has met with a loss in the death of this gentleman, not easily supplied. He has resided from his youth to the period of his death in this City, having witnessed its growth from a small village to a large and flourishing town, the center of a widely extended trade, and the terminus of railroads and canals, for whose completion he was a faithful and influential laborer." He was present at the "Old Settler's Meeting," held at Athens in 1854, and contributed much to the interest and instruction of the assembly. He died in 1863.

Newtown was called by that name when Sullivan's army passed through the country, which name was retained until by act of Legislature, in 1808, it was changed to Elmira. The village was incorporated in 1815. It has been a place of much business importance. The Elmira Female College, which was incorporated and opened in 1855, now ranks among the first collegiate institutions of the State. Elmira is now a beautiful City, containing 20,000 inhabitants.

Owego is charmingly situated on the Susquehanna River, near the creek from which it derives its name. The Owego Creek, meaning "Swift Water," was an important boundary with the Indians when they disposed of their lands lying on either side of it.

Mr. Draper purchased of the Indians a half

township east of the creek, embracing the site
where Owego now stands. The Indian name has
been retained with slight variation. The early
settlers spelled and called it Ah-wah-gah, which
Judge Avery considers more correct.

Owego and Elmira were half shire towns for
Tioga County until a Court House was built at
Spencer in 1812, where they held their courts for
this extensive county. The Court House was destroyed by fire in 1821, and in 1836 the county
was divided into Tioga and Chemung, Owego and
Elmira being the county seats.

The medicinal springs at Spencer are much
celebrated, and quite a place of resort for invalids.

The country below the village of Owego on the
Susquehanna, and below Elmira on the Tioga,
down to the State line, is interspersed with many
small villages, while schools and churches, which
always indicate improvement, have become numerous. A half century ago school houses were
generally built of logs, and barns and private
houses were used for churches. Many in the surrounding country will remember the crowds on
foot and horseback which might be seen passing
on their way up to the large barn of Samuel Ellis,
in Ellistown, or to the log dwelling of Mr. Hanna,
(who lived to be over one hundred years old).
The influence that spread from these early religious meetings was salutary and extensive, and the
spirit of them is felt by many now living.

Several young men among the Tozer and Ellis
families, together with a son of Judge Coryell, and
some others, became preachers of the gospel, and

have spent long lives of usefulness. Some years after, K. Elwell and T. Wilcox, of Milltown, were licensed as preachers of the gospel.

XVIII.

MILLTOWN.

LATE in the last century a street was laid out in the north part of Athens, on the ridge, extending up to the State line, and a settlement made which was called Milltown. The lots were large, and houses were built for a physician, a clothier, a tanner and shoemaker, blacksmith, carpenter, and deer skin leather dresser, which with the mills, store and public house, made it quite a business place.

The burying ground was laid out as it now is, and a large log schoolhouse erected upon it, which from its first opening was an institution of importance. Dr. Prentice, an educated and useful man, was the first teacher employed there. He removed his family from New London, Conn., to Pennsylvania in 1797. A house was built for him on the hill, near the creek, and a drug store connected with it; a part of the original building still remains.

He was one of the sufferers in New London at the time that City was burned by Arnold the traitor, in 1781, and continued there some years, in the practice of his profession. He was an uncle

of John Shepard, and much beloved by him.
There was no place of resort that afforded so
much pleasure as the house of Dr. Prentice, across
the way, where visitors were entertained with
books, interesting stories and ancient curiosities.
Among the latter were the bed curtains, painted
by Mrs. Prentice herself, on pure Irish linen.   On
the head curtain sat the King and Queen, crowned
with regal dignity, with fruits and flowers surrounding them.   On the side curtains were lesser
dignitaries, with vines and grapes and flowers. On
the valance was a vine extending the entire length,
with clusters of grapes, ripe plums and pears.
The work was neat and elegant, and the design
ingenious.   But what was more than all, their
crowning value was, that they were much scorched
and damaged at the time New London was burnt
by Arnold, the traitor, during the Revolution.

These were brought out only on extraordinary
occasions to entertain visitors and particular
friends.   An elegant toilet cover, also stitched with
the needle by this ingenious woman, and the
antique silver cup and elegant china punch bowls,
were among the curriosities exhibited, saved from
the wreck of Arnold's depredations.   Some of
them are yet to be seen in the possession of child-
dren's children.

Mrs. Prentice was the daughter of the Rev. Mr.
Owen, of Groton, a friend and cotemporary of
President Edwards.

Dr. Prentice practiced medicine in this country
several years.   He died suddenly, in August,
1805, much beloved and lamented.

His son, William, who was well educated, came
into this country in 1798. He had been admitted
to the bar in New London, and practiced law in
Lycoming County, at Williamsport. A little more
than a year after his father's death, on his return
from court, he was taken sick with fever at his
boarding house, (Squire Saltmarsh's,) went to his
home at Milltown, and died in a few days, in the
fall of 1806. He was a young man of good talents
and fine personal appearance. He wore his hair
braided, hanging on his shoulders, according to
the custom of the times. In his death the high
hopes of his family and friends were suddenly
blasted.

Dr. Prentice's eldest son was a physician, and
settled at Sag Harbor, on Long Island.

Another son was a tanner, and had an establishment a little above his father's, opposite the
residence of Mr. O. B. Spring. He went west
with his family many years ago.

· One of the daughters married Dan. Elwell, of
Westchester County, N. Y., a carpenter, who lived
many years at Milltown. They outlived the most
of their children. Some still living hold high
positions. The surviving daughter, who had the
care of her father many years, is living at Vanetten-
ville, where he died, April 19th, 1868, at the age
of 94 years. Mrs. Elwell died many years ago.

Dr. Prentice's second daughter married John
Spalding. He was first Sheriff of Bradford County,
and lived at Athens, opposite the village, until his
death.

The third daughter married J. F. Satterlee, who

was a merchant at Milltown, and afterward at Tioga Point, where Mrs. Satterlee died.

Mrs. Prentice was a lady of intelligence and of a cheerful temperament. When living alone, after her husband's death and children's marriages, she would often, notwithstanding her advanced age and bereavements, entertain her company by dressing herself in her rich damask, with long bodice waist and sleeves tight to the elbow, with wide lace ruffles and a long trail to her skirt, thrown over her arm, as was the style of her early days.

Dr. Spring succeeded Dr. Prentice as physician at Milltown. He also taught school a long time in connection with his practice.

The first school house was on the north side of the road, on the burying ground lot, near the present entrance. There the youth of that day were taught the rudiments of education, and many were graduated there. The school was sometimes visited by New England missionaries, who gave the pupils excellent instruction, and presented them with good books.

The school had been taught by Dr. Prentice, Amos Franklin, brother of Colonel Franklin, Dr. Satterlee, and several New England men of education and refinement.

But this seat of learning passed away suddenly. One morning early we were terrified by seeing it in flames, and the cumbrous logs one after another fell to the ground. Some business men from Philadelphia were once at Mr. Shepard's, when his young son, Isaac, was called upon to do the writing. "Where was your son educated?" inquired one of the gentlemen, when he saw his penmanship. Mr. Satterlee pointed to the log school house and said "it was there my son was educated."

Captain Thomas Wilcox came from Tyringham, Mass., near the beginning of this century, and settled at Milltown. He was a blacksmith by trade, and commenced life with small means. He purchased a valuable tract of land of Mrs. Shepard, for which he succeeded in paying by close application to his trade, and by transporting goods across the country from Catskill, bringing supplies of dyestuffs, machinery, and various articles for the mills. Mrs. Wilcox was a humble and devoted christian.

Francis Snechenberger was a German, who came from Philadelphia in 1799. He bought a lot of land in Milltown, containing about three acres. Mr. Snechenberger was a deer skin leather dresser. Loads of deer skins were taken to him, and there dressed and manufactured into mittens, moccasins and breeches, until a load was made out, which he peddled about the country, bringing home money and necessaries for his family. The day he was 70 years old he was drowned by falling into his spring.

His wife was an Irish woman, who sometimes entertained us with her adventures. In early life she left her home in Ireland, which did not suit her ambitious mind, and worked for her passage across the ocean. When she arrived at Philadelphia, she went first to the house where Major

Andre was imprisoned, a little previous to his execution. She understood the circumstances of his case, and her sympathies for him were greatly moved. She was afterwards directed to the house of Dr. Willson, and Katie became the nurse of the infant James P. Willson, subsequently the Rev. J. P. Willson, D. D., pastor of the First Presbyterian Church on Independence Square, Philadelphia, and predecessor of Rev. Albert Barnes.

According to her own story, she received much kindness and many favors from the good mother, "Madame Willson," yet sore offence did she give this honored lady, when on arriving at womanhood she yielded her consent to become the wife of Francis Snechenberger, a German, who fell in her way. When Katie timidly revealed the case to her mistress, the Madame, with much feeling, exclaimed, "Hang the men." She was loth to give up her faithful nurse and kind handmaid. Katie had been a great reader, and brought with her to this country a mind stored with royal lore. Kings and Queens, Princes and Dukes, with their retinues and historical peculiarities, were as familiar to her as her books and family inmates.

She had access to some medical works at Dr. Willson's, by which she acquired much knowledge of medicine. After her marriage she came to this place, and conceived the idea of becoming a female physician and nurse. She soon acquired celebrity and had an extensive practice. Some of her garden herbs still yield abundantly by the wayside. She had one daughter, who married William, son of Philip Cranse.

Another remarkable character was Mrs. Mead, said to have been a hundred years old when she died. She was a native of Dutchess County, and married a man much inferior to herself.

During the Revolutionary war the British came suddenly upon them and were about to take away her husband as prisoner. She affirmed that her husband was an idiot, and would be of no possible use to them, and must remain under her care. The argument prevailed, and she was ever after the sole director of their domestic affairs, which under the management of this energetic woman, afforded them a comfortable living. Her family made one of the first openings on the surrounding mountains, on a sightly spot back of Waverly, which is still called "Mead's hill."

Josiah Crocker removed from Lee, Mass., to Milltown in 1808, and engaged with Mr. Shepard in building a fulling mill and saw mill across the State line, on the Thomas tract. Carding machines were added afterwards.

Mr. Crocker had a large family of sons and two daughters, well trained after New England customs. The first object with him was to have the school house rebuilt. It is said that this good man when he went into the woods with his line and plummet knelt down by the first timber that was felled, and prayed that the house they were about to build might be one for the honor and glory of God and the good of the people. A snug school house was soon erected on the opposite side of the road from the old one, where the higher branches as well as rudiments were taught, and foundations laid for future development. Some distinguished men, both in Church and State, have received their education there. It also served as a church, and the then young and talented, now the aged and venerable Dr. Wisner, of Ithaca, first preached there and at the academy at "The Point" alternately, on the Sabbath, in 1812—15, but after serving two generations the house was demolished. The district having become reduced by the removal of families toward the Susquehanna River, another school house was built, near Wheelock's factory, which has superseded the old one of cherished memory. Mr. Crocker built a small house for himself on the ridge, near Factoryville, opposite the mill where he and his numerous boys were engaged in carding wool, dressing cloth and sawing lumber. The morning and evening sacrifices were daily offered there, and it was pleasant to see on the Sabbath this long train of neatly clad and well instructed children following their parents to the place of worship. They removed west in 1818.

The earliest record we have of the burying of the dead in this place, is that of the soldiers of General Sullivan, who fell in the battles with the tories and Indians at Chemung in 1779.

It is said that thirty of them were killed, but it is not known that more than six were brought to Tioga for interment. The presumption is there were more.

Mr. C. Stephens, whose family came here as early as 1788, says that the dead, both whites and Indians, were buried along the ridge, where the burying ground was laid out by the Connecticut settlers, and afterwards given to the town by Mr. Caton, the Pennsylvania claimant and proprietor. It is not known that Mr. Caton ever gave a formal deed.

The lot was fenced and many were buried there before the close of the eighteenth century.

It was at first enclosed by a splint rail fence. A brisk northwester once caused such vibration of the splinters as to produce a doleful moaning which some thought resembled the voice of an old Indian woman, who had recently been buried there, and her superstitious enemies verily thought she was coming again to take vengeance upon them. Some persons of courage ventured to investigate the mystery, and reported to the troubled ones— much to their relief. This was one of the legends of early days. As we enter this hallowed place, solemn and thrilling remembrances steal over us. Here are gathered the friends of early days, with whom we have "taken sweet counsel and walked to the house of God in company." Families in their narrow house here rest peacefully with only the cold marble and the dull earth to mark their possession. Men of business have here laid them down to rest, wearied of the turmoil of life, the fruitless greed of gain, and the ambition which rules, but never satisfies. Pastor and people, in a "Congregation which ne'er breaks up," are here assembled—faithful fathers and tender mothers, blooming daughters and noble sons, until the earth is moistened by tears and hallowed by sacred affection. Little children too are here, the music of their voices hushed, little feet tire, little hearts grieve no more, for "He who gathers the lambs with His arm and carries them in His bosom, has safely garnered them into His upper fold."

"There are treasures, deep hid in this mouldering earth,
Precious gems laid tenderly down."

"Who is that coffin for," said a young man as he entered a cabinet shop in this place. He was in the flush of youth and health, and gave promise of many years of life and labor. "It is for you," was the careless and jocose reply. "I am not ready for it yet," rejoined the youth. He was much nearer death, the coffin and the grave, than he then thought. In a few days he was seized with a violent fever, which in a short time terminated his career, and he was buried in the same coffin over which those thoughtless remarks were made so recently.

"Walk solemn on the silent shore
Of that vast ocean we must sail so soon."

A new cemetry has been recently opened on the Plains, which will be made both ornamental and attractive, but the old burying ground should be carefully guarded and sacredly venerated, as the resting place of those who have served their generation faithfully, and left to us so goodly a heritage.

The Milltown burying ground, in the north part of the town, was given to the public by John Shepard, Esq., in the last century.

He has been buried there many years, with nu-

merous descendants and friends around him.   The
ground has been neatly enclosed by Mr. O. B.
Spring, and ornamented with trees, giving additional beauty to the surrounding neighborhood.

From the first settlement of Athens, by the Connecticut people, their attention was given to the
education of their children.   As early as the survey of the township, in 1786, we find on a map of
that date public lands appropriated for that object.
This lot of several acres was situated north of
the Susquehanna Bridge road, the river on the
east, and the road leading to Milltown on the
west.   It was thickly covered with pines on the
north.   Soon after the settlement of the town the
first school house in the township was built on
this land, near the location of the present district
schoolhouse.

It was a small building of logs, suited to the
wants and circumstances of the inhabitants at that
time.   The first school was taught by Benedict
Satterlee.   He was a Connecticut man, of good
education and standing.   As the country became
settled, and a larger house was in demand, another schoolhouse was built on an improved plan, of
hewn logs ; on the street leading to Milltown.
This school was taught by Daniel and Elias Satterlee, brothers of Benedict.   Elias Satterlee afterward studied medicine and removed to Elmira.
Mr. Samuel Satterlee was also a man of education, and taught at Athens, and was at one time a
member of the Legislature.

This was the only literary institution for many
years.   It is said to have been a very good school.

This school house was burned early in the century. A school was afterward opened in the large log building formerly occupied by Mr. Alexander, on the cross street, north from Chemung bridge, and extending through the Paine lot, to the Susquehanna river.*

This was taught by a Mr. Thompson. The room was sometimes used for religious meetings, until the academy was in progress.

The old academy records, commencing with the date, Tioga, February 11th, 1797, have furnished the following account of its first commencement, written by Mr. Daniel Alexander, one of the earliest residents:

"Whereas, it is the earnest wish of many of the inhabitants of this town that a public building should be erected for the accommodation of an Academy, or seminary of learning for the accommodation of youth, and also be occasionally occupied as a place of public worship, or other public purposes; and whereas the erection of such a building on Tioga Point, and making other public improvements, would not only be of great use and convenience to the inhabitants, but would also have a tendency to enhance the value of land and other property, the subscribers to this agreement do therefore mutually covenant and agree to form themselves into an association for the purpose aforesaid, to be subject to the following regulations."

---

*No remains of this once important street are left. On it there have been two stores, a dwelling house, school room, and place for religious meetings, and near by a distillery, altogether making it quite a prominent street.

Then follows a series of resolutions, common upon the organization of such associations, fourteen in number.

The 12th resolution is, "the building contemplated shall be erected on one of the public lots in the township of Athens, on Tioga Point, and the construction thereof shall be as follows : It shall be forty-two feet in length, twenty-four in width, and two stories high. The second story shall be formed into one entire hall, to be arched and finished in a handsome manner."

Committee reported that they had decided upon a building lot. It was built by subscription, and divided into shares of thirty dollars each. The names of the subscribers, were Noah Murray, Sen., Chester Bingham, Joseph Spalding, Levi Thayer, David Alexander, Nathan Thayer, John Shepard, David Paine, Joseph Hitchcock, Elisha Mathewson, Ira Stephens, Elisha Satterlee, Samuel Campbell, John Spalding, Nathan Buel, Clement Paine, Julius Tozer, Jonathan Harris, Joseph Farlane, Daniel Satterlee, Simon Spalding, Thomas Overton, John Jenkins, George Wells, John Franklin, Warton Reid, Stephen Hopkins.

March 2d, 1797. At a meeting of the stockholders of Athens Academy, held agreeable to notification at the house of Captain Elisha Mathewson, on Thursday, March 2d, 1797, voted that Noah Murray, Esq., be chairman, that Clement Paine be secretary of this society. Voted, that Major Elisha Satterlee, Messrs. John Spalding and John Shepard, be trustees of this society. The name decided upon was that of the Athens Academical Society.

March 3d, 1798. Resolved, That this society will petition the Legislature for an act of incorporation, and also the grant of a lottery. Resolved, That the society will petition the Susquehanna Company, at their next meeting, for a grant of land, to be appropriated as a fund, for the said seminary of learning.

The frame was raised and enclosed, but the work dragged heavily. After raising the frame and making some progress, their funds were exhausted, and the building remained unfinished for a length of time, and was used, so tradition says, by merchants and others for storing surplus property or goods, and that it actually became a depository for hay, flax, skins, and the like articles. This kind of testimony, though not reliable, would seem in the present case to be corroborated by a petition on record in the archives of said institution, from the " proprietors" to the trustees, requesting them " to prevent any person whatever from putting hay, flax, or any other thing whatever in said building."

The fact that it remained for some length of time in a neglected condition gave occasion to apply to it the language of a traveling poet:

" Their only school house quite in ruin lies,
While pompous taverns all around them rise."

It must be confessed there was too much justice in the criticism in regard to the school house, but it may be averred the writer took quite a poetic liberty with the taverns.

May, 1808, they passed a resolution, and "authorized the trustees to advertise the academy for sale, to be sold on credit of twelve months, the purchaser giving judgment bonds with approved security."

July 20th, 1808, they "agreed that the vote ot May last, for selling said building, be rescinded and of no effect."

In 1809 "Clement Paine was requested to repair the building, and put the same in a good state of preservation, with a balance of one hundred and forty dollars due him, which he held as a lien on said building until paid."

The upper room of the academy was occupied by the Masonic society, and was under their control.

1813. In consequence of a petition of several members of the Athens Academical Society, presented to the Assembly of the Commonwealth of Pennsylvania, by Henry Welles, Esq., a member thereof from Athens, an act was passed giving the trustees of the academy full control of everything appertaining to it as an institution of learning, and a grant of $2,000 to the trustees of said academy, which should by them be invested in some safe and productive stock, the interest of which they should apply to the purposes of the institution. The academy to school four poor children, not exceeding two years each, gratis; provided there is application made for them. The act passed 27th February, 1813.

June 20th, 1813, Henry Welles was chosen trustee, to supply the vacancy caused by the death of George Wells, his father.

AN ORDER FROM THE TRUSTEES ON STATE TREAS-
URER.

July 10th, 1813. We have deputed Henry Wells, Esq., or order to receive the money from the State, and his receipt shall be an adequate voucher. John Franklin, Julius Tozer, Abner Murray, Stephen Hopkins, David Paine, John Saltmarsh, John Shepard, Clement Paine."

1814. Mr. Henry Wells recommended and engaged a young gentleman at Harrisburg for teacher, with a salary of five hundred dollars—Mr. Sylvanus Guernsey. Notice of school was advertised in the Wilkesbarre Gleaner and Towanda papers.

On Monday, the 25th of April, 1814, Mr. Gurnsey commenced the first school taught in the academy. Left March 6th, 1815.

In 1820 the trustees "voted that the funds appropriated by the State, amounting to $2,000, should be applied to aid the company for the erection of a bridge over the Tioga river."

March 5th, 1842, the academy was consumed by fire, together with quite a valuable library, philosophical apparatus and cabinet of curiosities.

In 1843 the academy was rebuilt, under the superintendence of H. W. Patrick, Esq., at a cost of $2,000.

In 1829 the bridge stock was sold to Judge Herrick.

NAMES OF PRECEPTORS AT DIFFERENT PERIODS.

Mr. Guernsey,	1814.	Mr. Baldwin,	1839-40.
Mr. Wells,	1815.	J. Marvin,	1840-41.
Nathaniel P. Talmadge,	1815.	Mr. Merchant,	1842.

Mr. Bush,.................. ....1815.	L. M. Pert,.......................1845.
Mr. Wellington,..........1816-17.	F. Hendrick,.....................1847.
Mr. Kee,.......................1818-19.	Rev. C. Thurston,.............1849.
L. Butler,.....................1822-23.	E· I. Ford,.......................1851.
Rev. J. Williamson,.........1824.	J. G. French,...................1852.
L. S. Ellsworth,.................1825.	A. Dunning,........... ....1852.
G. A Mix,.......................1825.	J. G. and Wm. French,.....1855.
E. Marsh,.......... ....1828.	J. S. Hopkins,................1856.
Ezra Stiles,.............1829-30-31.	F. Bixby,.................1859-60-61.
Dr. Wm. McDougal,.........1833.	J. M. Ely,..........1862-63-64-65.
D. M. Bennet,..................1835.	A. M. Loutrell,...........1866-67.
Bennet and Patrick,.........1836.	C. Mullock,.................1868-69.
A. Williams,................... 1837.	

XIX.

POSTOFFICE AND STAGES.

PREVIOUS to the opening of the new century, letters were conveyed by private individuals, and packages of letters were sent by the boats. It was sometimes attended with considerable labor to open and distribute these packages, which was always done at Hollenback's store. The mail was looked for as often as a boat arrived, and distributed with as much order as circumstances would permit.

No postoffice had been established at Athens until the summer of 1800, when Mr. William Prentice, son of Dr. Prentice, late of New London, received the appointment of postmaster. His office was in Hollenback's store. He was a young man of much promise, and his services in public life were held in high estimation. He acquited himself honorably for a little more than five years, when he died suddenly of fever. From this time there seems to have been no appointment made for two years. Col. Samuel Satterlee officiated pro tem, when Mr. David Paine was appointed postmaster in 1808, and served until 1818, when he was re-appointed, and continued post master until April, 1824, when he resigned in favor of D. A. Saltmarsh. Ebenezer Backus, appointed April 3d, 1827; Lemuel Ellsworth, 1831; John Judson, 1840; O. D. Satterlee, 1841; C. S. Park, 1844; C. H. Herrick, 1845; N. C. Harris, 1848; W. Olmsted, 1853; C. H. Herrick, 1856; Wm. Fritcher, 1861; S. B. Hoyt, incumbent, 1864.

Ebenezer Backus, Esq., was engaged for the government as traveling agent in the post-office department, and resided at Athens with his family many years. He married Miss Lindsley, a sister of Mrs. Dr. Hopkins. Soon after he came to Athens he bought what is now called the Backus house, of Jeremiah Decker built in 1816. The north wing, as it now is, was a part of the first farm house in this place, built by Dr. Hopkins, near the close of the last century. It was in this wing of the house that the Congregational church was formed in 1812. Mr. Backus had a large family of sons, and three daughters, two of whom married merchants of this place, Mr. Tompkins, who afterwards removed to Binghamton, and Mr. Ellsworth, who removed to Chicago. Mr. Backus was quite genial in his temperament, and this characteristic was hereditary in the family.

An early settler states that his first recollection of a mail carrier is of one Bart. Seely. For several years he made his appearance once a week on horseback, with a small mail bag. Then came Conrad Teter, who commenced carrying the mail in 1811 with a one horse wagon. He soon became the owner of two horses and a covered vehicle, and transported the mail several years from Wilkesbarre to Painted Post and back, once a week. After that he became the owner of a covered Jersey carriage, drawn by four horses, which ran between Wilkesbarre and Athens.

In 1814 Samuel Ovenshire commenced a line from Athens to Chenango Point, with a one horse wagon, which he ran for about three years.

In 1816 Conrad Teter went with his improved carriage and four horses to Owego, and started a line once a week from Owego to Newburg. It required two weeks to perform the trip. At the same time his brother-in-law Horton carried the mail for him, from Wilkesbarre to Athens. From thence to Painted Post it was carried by the Saltmarsh brothers.

In 1817 Justin Forbes commenced carrying the mail from Wilkesbarre to Athens, and continued four years.

About this time Stephen B. Leonard ran a stage with the mail from Owego to Painted Post by the way of Athens.

In 1820 the route from Wilkesbarre was extended to Ithaca. Mr. Forbes retained his interest in the rout to Wilkesbarre, and the Saltmarsh brothers ran a light two horse wagon from Athens to Ithaca.

In 1824 Forbes and Saltmarsh resumed the contract to Ithaca, until they went South to engage more extensively in carrying the mails.

In 1825 John Magee, of Bath, started a line with coaches twice a week from Owego to Bath. He was succeeded by his brother, and he by Cooley and Maxwell.

In 1849 the mails were first carried west by the Erie railroad, and stages no longer run north and south since the opening of the Southern railroad in 1867.

XX

SHAD FISHERY.

WITHIN the purchase of the Howel tract by Mr.
Shepard and Mr. Cranse, in 1806, there was a
beautiful island in the Susquehanna River, well
calculated for a fishery, and one was established
by them forthwith.

Mr. Cranse had the superintendence of it, and
in the spring of the year his family were much
occupied with making preparations for fishing.
Shad came up the river immediately after it was
cleared of ice. They were of the finest quality,
and in great abundance. They were caught on
the point of the island, nearly opposite Mr.
Cranse's door, and afforded entertainment to the
many spectators that gathered there to see the process of fishing, as well as profit to the fishermen.
First, a net two or three hundred yards long and
thirty-three meshes wide, made of strong linen
twine, with weights on one side and buoys on the
other, was taken into a large canoe. The canoe
was then pushed up the river half a mile, leaving
another canoe on the shore holding one end of the
seine, while the first pushed across the Susque-

hanna, the men letting off the seine as they crossed to the opposite shore ; when both moved silently down the river, pressing the unwary fish backward until they came to the island on either side, where was a general onset, the men jumping into the water, drawing up the seine, the fish floundering as they were thrown upon the point of the island by hundreds, and sometimes more than a thousand at a haul, while many by bounding over the net or breaking through it, would make a joyful escape.

Then came the process of dressing and dividing them among such as were entitled to their share, and often have the poor felt rich and the rich glad, as they carried home their several portions, with the prospect of having fresh shad for supper, and a supply for days to come. At one time the shad were so abundant that the fishermen agreed not to sell for less than three dollars a hundred, but a purchaser coming on the ground, a man who had a quantity for sale told him he could not sell them for less than three dollars, but he would give him a gross hundred—one hundred and twenty-five.

These shad came up the river in shoals, and the fishermen understood when they were approaching. Many barrels were packed in salt and sent to market.

This luxury had been the blessing of the red man from time immemorial, and of the white man for many years, until the dams in lower Pennsylvania were built, for the accommodation of the canals. The Susquehanna River shad were said to be equal to those of the Hudson and Connecti-

cut. There were other fisheries of some importance near this place—one on the Chemung River,
which sometimes yielded a bountiful supply.
Boys of former years, as well as of later days, will
always remember their fishing parties, and the
enthusiasm with which they have engaged in them
both day and night.

XXI.

TROY AND ADJACENT TOWNS

SUGAR Creek, a stream emptying into the Susquehanna at Towanda, formerly gave name to the region of country lying along its banks.

The Indian name, according to Mr. Maxwell, (who was interested in Indian history,) was "Oscoluwa." Conrad Weiser, a noted Indian interpreter, when on an embassy from the government to the Six Nations at Onondaga, in 1739, found the Indians living at the head waters of this stream destitute of food, and subsisting chiefly on the products of the maple tree, which they freely shared with him.

The banks of Lycoming and Sugar Creeks, approaching each other, were a thoroughfare for the Indians from the West to the north branches of the Susquehanna River, and after the natives were removed, the white people, following their track, found a promising and inviting country on these streams, and located farms, and established mills at a very early period.

Great quantities of maple sugar were made in this region, and also in Springfield and Smithfield, which, with the immense yield of native blackberries and other wild fruit, afforded luxuries which the early inhabitants of the more cultivated parts of the country did not enjoy.

But large and thriving villages are now springing up on the banks of these streams, and churches, schools and valuable machinery are indications of substantial improvement.

Troy, pleasantly situated on Sugar Creek, about twenty miles from its mouth, is a very flourishing village, containing many handsome buildings, and is a place of considerable thrift and importance. Among the first settlers were Smead, Rundel and Case.

Joseph Powel opened the first store in Troy, and an Englishman by the name of Philips kept the first tavern. The names of Ballard, Pomeroy and Long, are of later date.

A Baptist Church was erected here more than fifty years ago. This church has been well sustained, and is now the largest religious society in the place. Their Pastor, now 78 years of age, Elder Sheardown, is said to be a man of talent, and his labors have been much blessed during the long period of his ministry.

An institution of learning lately erected in Troy is an ornament to the place, and will do much toward promoting intelligence and refinement.

Numerous villages are springing up on the line of the Northern Central Railroad, between Elmira and Williamsport, which opens up the beauties of the country, and illustrates the truth of the stanza :

> " Where nothing dwelt but beasts of prey,
> Or men as fierce and wild as they,
> He bids the opprest and poor repair,
> And builds them towns and cities there."

Smithfield was an unbroken wilderness until about 1795, when the first permanent settlement is said to have been made by Reuben Mitchel.

In 1801 Samuel Kellogg, Nathan Fellows and Solomon Morse, of Poultney, Vermont, came to this uncultivated region and bought lands of the State for one dollar an acre, and settled with their families.

They were organized into a Congregational church before leaving Vermont. They had a little money, with which they purchased some supplies, which they brought with them, and when their resources failed, they were obliged to leave their families and go to a neighboring town, where provisions could be obtained.

Squire Kellogg, when 80 years old, related some incidents of his new country life. At one time he went away to work for bread, leaving as he thought a sufficient supply until he should return. He toiled hard about three weeks, earned twenty or thirty bushels of grain, and took it to Shepard's mills to be ground, then hired a team to carry it a part of the way home, where it was left on the river road in safe keeping until he could return for it. It was becoming dark, and he started for home on foot, through the dense forest, five or six miles. He arrived home about twelve o'clock at night, and found that his family had eaten their last morsel. Expecting her husband with a supply that night, the mother had borrowed a half a pint of Indian meal to make porridge. The children went supperless to bed ; the mother awaiting anxiously the sound of her husband's footsteps, and remembering her promise to the children, that when their father returned they should be fed. What was her dismay when he arrived, to find he had brought no supplies, and the weary father retraced his footsteps over this dreary way at midnight to provide food for his perishing family. Through the woods and snow, amid the howling of wild beasts, he went and came alone. He arrived home about daylight. The mother was watching and waiting, ready to prepare nourishment for the family, of which they partook with cheerful gratitude and a hearty relish.

The little church planted in Smithfield was like an "apple tree among the trees of the woods," which continued to grow and bear fruit. Rev. Seth Williston was one of the first missionaries among them.

About 1805 Nehemiah Tracy and family moved into the place, and gave much strength to the little church and community. There was soon a change in the appearance of the country. Stately trees bowed before these active woodmen, and in the openings here and there might be seen cheerful faces, domestic comforts, and abundance of wild fruit, together with any quantity of maple sugar, made by their own hands ; and more than all, the family altar was erected in every humble dwelling.

In 1812 they began to build a house of worship, which cost about three hundred dollars, and was accomplished by much effort. The lumber was drawn from the mills on the river, over a very rough road, and it was said that Nehemiah Tracy sold his last cow to buy nails and glass for the building. The house stood near the site of the present church. Rev. John Bascom was their first pastor ; he married the sister of Mrs. Clement Paine. Mr. Bascom died in Lansing, N. Y., where he was preaching, many years ago. His son, John Bascom, is a professor in Williams College. Mrs. Bascom is now living at Ludowville, N. Y., and is more than 80 years of age. Rev. William Franklin preached in Smithfield five or six years, and died there. Rev. C. C. Corss has been their pastor many years.

The articles for the Congregational church of Smithfield were drawn up by the Rev. Lemuel Haines, a distinguished colored preacher, at the time of its formation in Poultney, before the members emigrated to this country. This certificate reads thus :

" Samuel Kellogg, Esq. Solomon Morse and Nathan Fellows, having manifested a desire to be dismissed from the particular watch and care of this church, and to unite in a distinct church, being about to remove to Smithfield, Pennsylvania, County of Luzerne, (Bradford). The church accordingly voting their dismission ; they took upon them the solemn covenant of the Church, chose Mr. Kellogg their moderator and clerk, and were commended to God by prayer.

"The subscribers being present and assisting them in the solemn transaction.

" ELIJAH NORTON,
" LEMUEL HAINES,
Ministers of the Gospel.
"POULTNEY, Vt., February 11, 1801."

Mr. Haines was pastor of the principal Congregational church in Poultney, and afterward in Rutland, Vt., over which he presided many years; much respected and beloved for his good sense and Godliness.

Rev. Dr. Sprague, of Albany, in his "Lives of eminent New England Divines," speaks thus of Mr. Haines:

" Rev. Lemuel Haines was a minister of color, and the most eminent negro preacher ever known in this country. He was the pastor of intelligent churches. In spite of all he had to contend with, he became a man of mark, respected for his piety, talents and usefulness, and was admired for his keen and ready wit."

A physician of loose principles in a contiguous town was about to remove to a distant part of the country. As he passed through Rutland, where Mr. Haines lived, they met. Mr. Haines said to him, " Doctor I am owing you a small debt and want to pay you." The doctor said to him, "Mr. Haines you have been a faithful preacher, and received but little support, I give you the debt," but continued, " you must pray for me and make a good man of me." Mr. Haines quickly replied, " Why Doctor, I think it would be easier to pay the debt."

Springfield, south of Smithfield, was named by settlers from Springfield, Mass. It was formerly called Murraysfield, for Noah Murray, whose descendants live in this region. He purchased a large tract of land adjoining Smithfield, and gave name to the town, and died there about 1812.

Ridgeway lies on the northern boundary of the State, directly west of Athens, and is about the same size. Much of the land was originally covered with pine timber, which has been converted into lumber, and sold at very small prices. There is now in the township a very respectable Irish settlement. Thirty or forty years ago some of the Irish laborers on the Erie canal were induced to buy lands in that place. Many of them went there and commenced clearing the woods. They were very prudent and industrious, and by dint of hard labor and severe economy, some of them have become quite extensive land owners.

Litchfield township was surveyed about 1795. John Pierce, father of Jack Pierce, who was deaf and dumb, and well known hereabouts, gave the name to Litchfield, after the town of the same name in Connecticut. Thomas Park was the first settler, in 1795. Samuel Park was the first child born in the town.

J. D. Leray de Chaumont, a Frenchman, was a Pennsylvania landholder, and owned a great part of Litchfield, and a considerable part of Athens, east of the Susquehanna. Colonel Kingsbury, who was his agent, was extensively known among the early settlers, and sold to the people in Athens their back lands at State prices—about three dollars per acre.

Eleazer and Solomon Merrill came to Litchfield from a county of the same name in Connecticut, in 1803. They came for the purpose of locating bounty land due their father, Eleazer Merrill, who was a soldier in the war of the Revolution. They settled on an elevated spot in Litchfield, near the Susquehanna River, made an opening in the forest, built a log cabin near a spring of choice water, and after a season of hard labor preparatory to bringing their families, they returned to Connecticut. It was a long and wearisome journey in those days, but they braved it through, and returned to their place of destination in Pennsylvania. They all ascended the mountain, the aged father and mother, sons and wives, and numerous children, and entered the humble dwelling that had been provided for them. Soon they branched out into other homes.

Being provident, they brought with them sundry comforts, a variety of seeds for planting, even flower seeds, which literally made the wilderness to blossom as the rose ; and a little money for necessaries, to serve them until their corn began to grow. They found the wild deer in abundance, and a variety of game and berries, affording them food and luxuries. The location has proved to be favorable to the families. Some of them are now said to be wealthy.

Fifty years have made a great change in Litchfield. It is now settled by many prosperous farmers and valuable inhabitants, with good

schools and churches.   Lands which were then
sold for three dollars are now worth twenty-five
dollars per acre, perhaps more.

XXII.

FACTORYVILLE AND WAVERLY.

FACTORYVILLE, in the town of Barton, * received its name from the mills that were erected there in the early part of the century. First a fulling mill, carding machines, and saw mill, by Messrs. Shepard and Crocker in 1809; then a factory by Messrs. Isaac and Job Shepard, afterwards bought and enlarged by Mr. A. Brooks. This was consumed by fire in 1853. A tannery is now in operation on the same ground. Another tannery just across the State line was established by Jerry Adams about fifty years ago, and is now owned by Stone and Perkins.

---

* The town of Barton was taken from Tioga, March, 1824, extending on the State line from the Susquehanna to the Tioga River. The names of the pioneers near the Susquehanna River were Ellis, Mills, Saunders and Hanna The latter lived to be over one hundred years of age. The early settlers on Shepard's Creek were Hedges, Barnes, Newel, Lyon, Bingham and English. Blackberries and maple sugar were abundant, and furnished partial sustenance to the inhabitants. These early settlers were principally from New England, and were among the most industrious and reliable people. The Ithaca turnpike, made in 1821, was a great advantage to them

A survey of Factoryville was made in 1819, by Major Flower, from the State line to George Walker's. The Ithaca turnpike was made in 1821, and the Owego and Chemung road opened about the same time.

A Postoffice was established in 1812; first at the factory, and afterward removed to Mr. I. Shepard's store, on the Owego and Chemung road.

The district was divided into large lots of land by John Shepard, Esq., and sold, reserving a number of acres for the mill lot, to Thomas Willcox, Moses and Elisha Larnard. These lots were again divided into village lots, which were sold, and neat and comfortable dwellings erected, and it is now a pleasant and thriving village.

Mr. John Barker was a gentleman of intelligence and refinement, cheerful and agreeable. His society was much sought, and he was beloved and respected by all. He came from Durham, N. Y., in 1830, to settle the estate of his nephew, young Hotchkiss, a merchant who had established himself at Factoryville a short time before, and died suddenly of a fever.

Mr. Barker continued the business and became a citizen. He married a sister of Mrs. Isaac Shepard, and they were pleasantly situated in Factoryville, when death removed the daughter, husband and son, in a few successive years. Mr. Barker died in New York City, 1855.

John Hotchkiss, a younger brother of the early merchant, was a clerk for Mr. Barker many years. Industrious and enterprising, he went to California, was successful in business, came home and was married, returned again, and died of yellow fever on his passage back to California, in 1853.

Mrs. Larnard, who resided many years at Factoryville, is a lady in whom refinement of manners, good sense and devoted piety are happily combined, and is still living at an advanced age.

The first Presbyterian Church of Factoryville was formed in the spring of 1847, eighteen of its members receiving letters from the Church of Athens. The Methodist and Baptist Churches were formed there a little previous. The Episcopal Church was formed and house built about 1853. These churches are now all located in Waverly.

Waverly is also in the town of Barton. In 1796 Mr. John Shepard purchased of General Thomas, of Westchester County, N. Y., one thousand acres of land at five dollars per acre, extending along the State line from Shepard's Creek at Factoryville, near the 59th mile stone, to 60th mile stone; thence across the north end of Spanish Hill to the Chemung River, and from the Narrows across the mountain beyond Shepard's Creek; thence down to the State line again, embracing Waverly, Factoryville, and many fine localities back of these villages, as has been already stated.

This tract was an entire wilderness at this time, except the flats and a few openings near them where the red man had tilled his corn a few years previous, and it had made a charming home for the wild deer and many other inoffensive animals, which herded and grazed, and roamed through the forest, and drank from the waters of the rivers and the pure springs from the mountain. The venomous rattlesnake was sometimes seen in numbers, but these reptiles, like the savages, have disappeared before the improvements of the white man.

In 1819 Deacon Ephraim Strong bought one hundred and fifty-three and one-half acres of land on this tract, just across the State line, one hundred rods in width, about an equal distance between Shepard's Creek and Chemung River, and extending back to the mountain.

Here Mr. Strong, with his numerous sons, made an opening in the pines, of several acres; planted corn and potatoes, sowed buckwheat, built a snug frame house, dug a well and set out an orchard. Some of the trees are still standing on the lot now occupied by Mr. Fuller.

Here this godly, intelligent and well educated household, the father a graduate of Yale College, and the mother a superior woman, lived several years. It was a privilege to call on this family and learn how to live and enjoy the comforts of a retired life, and look into their well read library, and hear this priest of his own family in the solitude of the forest offer the morning and evening sacrifice. Scott's Commentary was Mrs. Strong's principal reading, and in her obituary, many years after, it was said that she had read this work through seven times. The family removed to Hudson, Ohio, where many of them have died.

About 1825 Mr. Shepard paid Mr. Strong for his improvements and sold the land to General Welles. Shortly after November 1st, 1835, Mr. John Spalding, of Athens, bought the farm.

One of the "old fields" adjoining this farm on the west, extended from the locality where Mr. Waldo's drug store now is to the spot near where the depot stands, north of the State line, and is the ground on which the west part of Waverly is built. The other field was on the Pennsylvania side, where South Waverly stands. The old road from Milltown to Chemung formerly passed between the old fields. There is a tradition that the old fields were cultivated by the Aborigines, and they were sometimes called the "Indian Fields." These fields were very familiar to the early settlers, and their animals were often pastured there from some distance.

The public road was opened from Barton to Chemung through these lands and the lands of Isaac and Job Shepard, and a gradual improvement made. In 1846 Mr. E. Brigham built a hotel where the Methodist Church now is, which he called the Waverly House. The street running south from there was opened soon after, which was called Waverly street.

A few buildings had been erected in anticipation of a future village, and a Presbyterian Church was built in 1848. The lot was given to the congregation by Mr. Owen Spalding.

The Erie Railway now being constructed and fast approaching, the village began to grow rapidly, and many dwellings and stores were in progress, and in the fall of 1849 the Railway reached this point. A depot was built, and soon the sound of the engine whistle and the rattling of the cars announced their arrival at the newly made village, animating and cheering the expectant inhabitants.

The village was incorporated in 1854, and re-ceived the name of Waverly. A few votes more would have given it the name of Loder. Since that time Waverly has had a very rapid growth. The business of the place has constantly increased, and now its busy streets, its churches, banks, printing offices and other mechanical establish-ments, its stores, and an institute of learning of high standing, all give unmistakable evidence of thrift and prosperity. *

The early purchaser of this valuable tract of land once said, "It would not be surprising if at some future time you should see the spires of ten or a dozen churches between these rivers," and five or six are seen already in Waverly alone ; and in a little more than twenty years a village of more than 3,000 inhabitants has sprung up on this ground.

Spanish Hill lies a little west of Waverly. It is disrobed of much of its foliage, and divested of its crowning beauty—the ancient and mysterious fortifications on its summit. It lies principally in Athens, and has been described there.

The Postoffice was established in Waverly in 1849 ; the first great fire in March, 1855 ; Waverly Bank chartered 1855 ; Waverly Institute built 1857 ; First National Bank chartered 1863.

---

* Near the village, on Shepard's Creek, are the Waverly Paper Mills, erected in 1867, and now principally owned by Messrs. W. W. and C. H. Shepard, to whom we are indebted for the material upon which this volume is printed.

XXIII.

REMARKABLE EVENTS.

AFTER the destruction, by a worm, of the large
yellow pine trees of the last century, and the
new trees had sprung up and were clothed with
verdure, the locusts appeared in 1800 and devoured
every green thing before them. At first a worm
that worked itself out of the earth in vast numbers
appeared. The ground was alive with them. A
shell next formed, which after a little time, opened
on the back and the locust came out with wings
and legs, resembling the grasshopper, but much
larger. They soon flew to the trees and bushes
in multitudes, and devoured the foliage. They
passed off the same season, but came again in
1814, which many now living very well remember.
The singing of the locusts in the pine plains above
the village of Athens made it difficult to hear conversation by the way. They nearly all left the same
season. American locusts are said to resemble
those of the eastern hemisphere, but are not so
large.

The total eclipse of 1806 is remembered by
many now living as a grand and sublime scene, a

recurrence of which is not expected in this longitude during the present generation. The late eclipse of August 7th, 1869, approached nearer to it than any other we have witnessed, and a few degrees west of us the sun's disk was entirely obscured.

A grand celestial phenomenon, a meteoric shower, was exhibited in the heavens, on Thursday morning, the 13th of November, 1833, between the hours of two and five o'clock, and was witnessed by many people in this part of the country, and in this village, as well as through the country generally. Those who were fortunate enough to be up at that hour in the morning spoke of it as brilliant beyond description. It is a phenomenon that is fully substantiated by astronomers as occurring periodically, though not always visible to the same extent, in the same place. Some suppose there is a region in the space through which the earth passes in its orbit, where such meteoric scenes continually prevail, and more or less may be seen every year in November, about the 12th or 13th. The newspapers throughout the land contained notices of it under the caption, "Remarkable Phenomenon," "Extraordinary Phenomenon," "Falling Stars." One writer remarked, "the shooting stars were harmless, and as a general thing vanished before they reached the earth."

Another remarkable scene was witnessed in 1838. An annular eclipse of the sun, as predicted by astronomers; when a most beautiful luminous ring was seen in the heavens while the moon appeared on the centre of the sun's disk.

These unusual events strike us with wonder, while the ordinary exhibitions of the heavenly bodies make but little impression.

> " The glorious Architect,
> This, His universal temple, hung
> With lustres, with innumerable lights—
> Let not man withhold his homage."

XXIV.

IMPROVEMENTS.

WHEN our fathers first came to Tioga Point there were no roads for the white man. An Indian trail, following the river banks, was the only opening through the thick pines. These paths, with the river itself, had afforded the only facilities for traveling. They were used only by footmen, the river was navigated by means of the "light canoe." With a little improvement these Indian roads were used by the white people for many years. When the first survey of this town was made a road was laid out nearly in its present course from Athens to Milltown. The most direct route for the traveller, or the mail from Owego to Newtown, was by the way of Tioga Point, until about 1821, when a road was opened from the Susquehanna, via Factoryville, to the Chemung river, thereby leaving Tioga Point out of the accustomed route of travel, considerably to its disadvantage. A private road had been opened from Milltown through the thick pines to Chemung, which was also much used by travellers, and afterwards became a public road. The cir-

cuit from Tioga Point to Milltown, thence across
to the Chemung, and down the river to the village
again, affords a very pleasant ride. A few gay
young men of former times once tried it on a Sunday in a lumber sleigh filled with straw. They
scattered the straw as they rode along in their
merriment, and thus the route obtained the name
of "the straw line," by which it has been called
ever since. It is said that complaint was entered
against them, and they suffered the penalty for the
violation of law.

Modes of traveling and conveyance were very
different in former times from the present. Canals,
railroads, steamboats, and even stage coaches,
were unknown at the beginning of this century.
It was common to see the footman travelling with
his knapsack on his back. Riding on horseback
was the common mode of conveyance from place
to place, and even of making long journeys.
Sometimes a gentleman and lady, or a father and
mother with two children, might be seen pursuing
their way in this style.* Another very safe meth-
od of travelling was by means of oxen attached to
a cart or sled, and often whole families were conveyed in this way to a social gathering, or to the
place of worship. Long trains of emigrants thus
pursued their way to Alleghany or Ohio. As the
country improved a chaise or gig was occasional-

---

* It is related that "a bridal party from Catharinestown, on Seneca lake, visited Tioga Point, in 1793, on horseback, to find the
nearest justice authorized to perform the ceremony." The magistrate was probably Noah Murray, Esq., father of the late Noah
Murray, well known in Athens.

ly seen, and in due time, wagons, stages and coaches were introduced.

Parties to a hymenial engagement might sometimes be seen wending their way on horseback to the house of the minister or magistrate. My father being a magistrate, wedding ceremonies were often performed at his house. The parties generally came without attendants, and frequently both riding one horse. One cold and blustering December day, when the doors were closed and the family gathered around a large fire, a sprightly young man with his espoused helpmeet alighted at the door and inquired for Squire Shepard. The object was soon disclosed to the Squire, and readily understood by the family, when every other engagement yielded to the occasion in hand. The nuptials were soon solemnized, and the groom and bride were ready for their departure. A white dress and thin shawl were the only protection of the lady from the inclemency of the weather, and as she stood upon the horseblock awaiting the movements of her spouse, with the wind whistling through her garments, she exclaimed, "why Philander I shall freeze." "Oh, no," said he in blandest tones, "that would not be consistent," and soon they rode rapidly away with colors flying. Squire Shepard never required a fee for performing a marriage ceremony. Morever it was his practice to present the bride with a Bible, desiring her to make it the guide of her life.

Athens, or Tioga Point, was formerly noted for the number of its distilleries, there having been at one time not less than six or seven in operation at once. The first one of the last century was built of logs on the back part of the lot where we uow live. The well for the distillery, and now in use, was dug by Daniel Moore, a Hessian, who remained in the country after the close of the revolutionary war. The well was in a dilapidated condition, and remains of the pump that had been used were still in it when we came into possession of the lot. The distillery was carried on for many years by Daniel Alexander, and was then a lucrative business and considered reputable. The degraded whites and Indians who still remained in the country were there supplied with whiskey. Another in the north part of the village succeeded this, on an improved plan, having a windmill connected with it for grinding the grain. There was another at Milltown, and another still at Chemung Narrows. As these began to run down, three or four more were started on the west side of the Chemung river, and two on the east side of the Susquehanna river, all in this town, and were in full operation many years, when the temperance movement seemed to affect them unfavorably, and they tottered and fell. The whiskey now used at Athens is altogether supplied from other places, none being manufactured in the place or vicinity.

The effect of the failure of these distilleries has been a decided improvement in the cause of temperance, and we may expect that when foreign supplies cease temperance will triumph.

A most striking instance of the effects of intemperance was the case of Moses Roberts, a graduate of Yale College. He came to this country about the close of the last century, and bought a farm in Athens, became an inebriate, and sank step by step to a stupid sot. He married an imbecile woman, became demented himself, his farm was sold, his children bound out, and for many years he made splint brooms for a living. He died near a distillery, and was buried as a town pauper in 1824.

The Pennsylvania canal was surveyed through this part of the State by Mr. Randall, Chief Engineer, about the year 1830, and went into operation in 1854. Much of the lumber and other property that was formerly run on the river, now finds a surer and safer conveyance by the canal. Large quantities of coal from our mining regions are transported by the canal to market in the northern part of the State, and in the State of New York.

The Pennsylvania and New York railroad was surveyed in the summer of 1866. The first train entered the village from Towanda, November 26th, 1867. Regular trips on the road, from New York, were commenced September 20th, 1869, thus facilitating travel along the river, and affording to the passenger a marked contrast to the previous mode, over a very hilly and winding road. We can now sit by our fireside and hear the whistle and rattle of the Erie trains, and can see trains on the North Pennsylvania railroad, many times in a day, as they pass along with whistle and echo. These with the foundry and tannery, make a combination of sounds evincing substantial and cheering improvement.

A bridge over the Chemung river was built in 1820, and rebuilt in 1836. Another, and much longer and more expensive one over the Susquehanna, was built in the year 1841. A bridge over the Chemung, at "Tozer's", was built about the same time.

These bridges take the place of the ferries of former times, which were often difficult and sometimes dangerous to pass.

In 1844 it was announced in the public prints that Professor Morse had discovered a plan, by the aid of electricity, to send messages from place to place, with a speed exceeding anything before known. He applied to Congress for aid to make trial of his invention, on a line between Baltimore and Washington city, which was granted him. It was soon put in operation. Now the novelty is passed, and we with other towns can readily avail ourselves of telegraphic facilities.

XXV.

THE DEER HUNT OF 1818.

"Up men ! arouse for the chase !
  The wild buck is quitting his lair,
The hills are gilded with light,
  And there's health in the balmy air."

WHEN the New York and Pennsylvania boys engaged in a grand deer hunt in this beautiful valley, in the fall of 1818, it was a gala day, such as they seldom enjoyed. The necessary plans and arrangements had all been matured. Fires had been lighted on the North Mountains the previous night, and the hounds sent out early to drive the deer down to the plains. Marshals for the day had been chosen to lead their respective bands. The appointed day anxiously looked for arrived, when about two hundred men, armed with guns and rifles, sallied forth from their homes in the early morning to engage in the exciting sport. A circle of men, of several miles in extent, was to be formed on the broad plains between the Susquehanna and Chemung rivers, extending beyond the hills on the north, and to the southern limit of the pine woods toward the South. They

were to move in uniform time and regular order,
toward one common centre, driving before them
the deer that traversed the plains and hills, and
were thus surrounded by the hunters, or hemmed
in by the rivers. Many have doubtless been the
joyous and frolicsome days of the sons of the
forest, when with their simple bow and arrow,
they sallied forth in numbers, and traversed the
same ground for the same object. The Indian and
his game have long since passed away from these
scenes, before the resistless march of civilation,
and they must now be sought toward the "setting
sun."

But to the hunt. The marshals of the day, at
the head of their respective commands, and clothed with due authority for the occasion, mounted
their steeds and rode forth at early dawn, each
having under command about one hundred men.
Mr. Elias Mathewson, leading the Pennsylvanians,
posted his men along the borders of the pine forest below the Mile Hill, extending his line from
river to river, about two miles above the junction
of the two streams.

The line of the New York men was stretched
from the Chemung river, near Buckville, across
the hills to Shepard's creek, on the north, all being at their posts, and in due order and readiness.
At the appointed time the march commenced.
Highly excited, the men on both sides pressed forward, eager for the game, watching every hillock
and glen, and scouring every thicket that might
serve as a hiding place for the deer. Often a
lusty buck was started from his retreat. Here

and there through the forest the timid doe and
fawn might be seen darting away from their pur-
suers, who still urging them forward from every
quarter, were driving and pressing them toward
the place of rendezvous, a point not far from the
centre of the present village of Waverly. Occasionally an animal more fortunate than the rest
would break through the ring, and make his
escape, but this only added to the excitement and
eagerness of the hunters. The men were not to
shoot any of the game, until orders were given.
But now the lines close in as they approach the
rendezvous from every side. Quite a number of
deer are discovered to be within the ring—excitement is at its height, and orders are given to fire.
The woods ring with the report of the musket and
the crack of the rifle. Many a noble buck is
brought down. Some of them stand at bay for a
while, but all in vain ; while the cringing doe and
helpless fawn become an easy prey to the pitiless
foe, who give no quarter at such a time. As they
approached the centre of the ring (said to be near
where the Waverly foundry now stands), the excitement increased to rashness and recklessness.
In their great anxiety to secure the whole of the
game, the hunters shot in every direction.

"In the heat of excitement men do not stop to
consider," and suddenly it was announced that a
man was wounded. This arrested the attention of
all for a time, such an interlude not having been
in the programme. The marshals ordered a cessa-
tion of firing, and the eager inquiry "who is it,"
went round the circle. The unfortunate hunter

thought himself desperately, if not fatally wounded, and the woods resounded with his piteous cries. Great was the consternation, and deep the sympathy among his friends and neighbors. The surgeon examined the wound with great caution, and not a little of anxiety. As he removed the garments, anxious friends were relieved upon ascertaining that it was not a serious wound ; indeed it proved to be rather a slight one, from which the man soon recovered. "Big Decker" also narrowly escaped being shot, a ball having struck a tree where he was standing, about six inches over his head. His ire being a little aroused, he asked to borrow a gun, having none of his own, to return the fire. But better counsels prevailed, and all was calm again. The business of the day had not yet come to an end. There were about thirty slaughtered animals to be cared for still, skinned, dressed and divided among the men, that each might have his due share of the spoils and results of the day. This was the drudgery of the hour, but skilled hands applied themselves to the work with a will, and it was soon accomplished. Distribution was then made of a part, the remainder sold at vendue, and the men dispersed to their several homes, glad to rest, and with the coming of the night all was quiet and still.

Such were among the sports and recreations of the dwellers in this valley half a century ago. Those who remain among us still, delight to recount the feats of skill and daring performed by them in their youth and early manhood in the various methods of hunting the deer, both by day

and by night. Some of their encounters with the
deer were not without considerable peril, though
for the most part, hunting was regarded only as a
pastime.

At an early day, and for some time subsequent
to the first settlement of the country, the deer
were quite numerous. Often might they be seen
bounding along their path, or turning to gaze at
the passing traveller. We have seen a little solitary fawn pursued by the dogs, almost to our very
door, and have often watched them grazing on the
fields of green wheat not far from our home, and
could scarcely begrudge them their delicious repast. Hunting the deer was quite a business with
a certain class, and their skins were among the
articles of trade with the merchant. Venison was
a very important article of sustenance, and when
corned or jerked could be kept any length of time.
The game from these forests and the fish from the
rivers afforded the aborigines almost indispensable
means of subsistence.

XXVI.

SOLDIERS.

AT the time of the Declaration of Independence, in 1776, the soil of Athens had scarcely been trod by the white man. Traders had occasionally passed through the valley, and it is said that a partial survey of the township was made as early as 1777, by John Jenkins, the noted and fearless surveyor of the Susquehanna Company. But soon after that time, the tories assembled here and at Chemung in great numbers, and planned their fiendish designs against Wyoming.

Several companies had been raised for the Continental service from the lower part of the valley, much to the disadvantage of the inhabitants, leaving them unprotected from British and savage ferocity combined, which overwhelmed them in 1778.

Many of the old soldiers, after the close of the war, removed from Wyoming up the river, and quite a number located in and about this place, then called Tioga Point. We remember some of the aged veterans, and should like to record the names of them all if they could be obtained.

Several soldiers and some prominent officers settled at Sheshequin. Many of them lie in our burying places. Colonel Franklin and Major Flower were buried on their farms across the river.

It was a custom with the merchants of the place to collect from the government the pensions of these aged soldiers, making advances to them in goods, provisions, etc., and when they assembled annually for a settlement, and to greet each other, to give them an entertainment at the hotel. On such occasions they sometimes assembled at the place of public worship to hear an appropriate discourse. There was an agreement between two of these veterans, Archy Temple and Solomon Talliday, that when the first died the survivor should fire a volley over his grave, which was fulfilled to the letter.

Military customs were kept up by our people from the earliest settlement. Regular seasons for drilling were observed, and at the time appointed for general training the various companies collected on parade, with martial music to enliven the scene. "A light horse company," so-called, with uniform of blue and red, with flowing sashes and nodding plumes, made a specially fine appearance on their noble steeds. When called upon, in 1812, to resist British aggression again, they were somewhat prepared for the conflict. Several volunteer companies went from this region to the Canada lines, the seat of war.

Captain Julius Tozer, with three of his sons, Julius, Samuel and Guy, were among the number; together with Elishama Tozer, Daniel Satterlee, John Brown, William Drown, Samuel Baldwin, several of the name of Wilson, four named Ellis, and several from neighboring towns; all attached to the regiment of Colonel Dobbins. The effect of this war was not felt so much in this part of the country as in many other places, except by the soldiers themselves, and its influence upon prices, which were marvellously high. When it was announced in the newspapers, in December, 1815, that peace had been proclaimed, and confirmed by the arrival of Coonrod Teter, the driver and proprietor of the weekly stage, with his white flag flying, it was a time of great rejoicing, and Athens was brightly illuminated at night, and the merry sleigh bells were sounding in the street till a late hour of that cold December night.

The nation was less prepared for war in 1861. There had been a long period of uninterrupted peace. The militia system was in bad repute generally. In this place, and in many parts of our country, it had been treated with ridicule and contempt. It had come to be considered so incompatible with the genius of our civil institutions, that militia drills and parades were no longer witnessed. The feeling of security was such that military matters were very unpopular, and all attention to them considered an unnecessary expense of time and money. The present generation had not heard the sound of war or battle. We were at peace among ourselves and with other nations, and when the attack was made upon Fort Sumter, in April, 1861, and the proclamation of the President was issued, calling for 75,000 men, to hasten to Wash-

ington, for the defense of the Capital and the
government, we were but poorly prepared to meet
the emergency.   Men of peaceable and quiet habits
of life, aroused by the necessities of the case, began to ask what they could do for their country,
and boys, too, whose enquiring minds had led
them to examine military books, were inspired
with a martial spirit, and offered themselves will-
ingly in response to the call.   They left their·
peaceful homes and joined the army, where they
found themselves subjected to many discomforts
and deprivations, but they were not forgotten by
friends who remained at home.   From the commencement of the war, many supplies were sent
from time to time by the ladies of Athens to their
sons and brothers, of which no account was kept.
But on the 30th of May, 1864, the ladies met at
the basement of the Episcopal church, for the purpose of forming a society to aid the Christian Commission.   After the election of officers, it was resolved to divide the town into districts, and ap-
point a committee of sixteen to solicit contributions monthly to the Ladies' Aid Society, auxiliary
to the American Christian Commission, for the relief and benefit of the soldiers.   The society went
into successful operation, and the object was faithfully followed up until the close of the war.   The
money raised that year by this society amounted
to $638, besides thirty-three boxes sent by the so-
ciety and individuals.   The bounty money for
soldiers raised by taxation in the borough of
Athens amounted to $15,100, and besides these
sums, other contributions were made by the people

for the benefit of the soldiers ; thus showing their sympathy for the cause of their common country.

The firing on Fort Sumter and the President's proclamation calling to arms were in April. The first company was raised at Athens in May, and reported at Harrisburg, commanded by Captain William Bradbury, Company F, Sixth Regiment Pennsylvania Reserves. The following is a list of the men belonging to Captain Bradbury's company: Captain, Wm. Bradbury ; 1st Lieutenant, L. D. Forrest ; 2d Lieutenant, W. A. Meeker. Sergeants —1st. William S. Briggs, 2d. Horace W. Perkins, 3d. G. F. Kinney, 4th. Myron Low,† 5th. Marshall O. Hicks. Corporals—1st. O. D. Lyons, 2d. George Perkins Rogers,* 3d. George L. Gardner, 4th. Silas J. Fritcher, 5th. Samuel S. Baker, 6th. Jeremiah French, 7th. John W. Schouten, 8th. William Langford.* Privates—Orlando Benson,* Patrick Burk,‡ Jason F. Bloodgood, William Boughton, Eben Brown, Edward Brigham, Enbulus Brigham, Thomas Barney,‡ Charles E. Brown, Franklin M. Cole, Samuel W. Cole, John P. Coleman, F. D. Campbell, Nathaniel Campbell, W. M. Chapman, Stephen Crayon, William Crayon, James Cooper, Benjamin M. Clark, Aaron Daily, James E. Demarest, Elijah DeCroff, Cornelius Driscoll, Dennis Drummy, Malcom H. Droyce,* Walter Farnsworth, Charley F. Fuller, John F. Flinn,* Orison Forest, Lorin W. Forest, William Foran, Joseph French, S. G. French,

---

† Killed at Antietam.
‡ Killed at Fredericksburg.
* Promoted to Sergeant.

Bennett French, Truman E. French, Owen Finlan, Alfred H. Forest, James R. Fox, Gordon Wellington,† Julius M. Hughes,‖ Michael Heavener, Sevellan Hicks, James E. Hall, Isaac Jones, Richard King, Horace Keeler, John Keyser, Orrin D. S. Kinney, C. S. Kinney, Flemming T. Lent, William Murray, John Munn, Tilden Munn, C. B. McNannon, Charles Merritt, Michael Moughan, Alfred D. C. Miller, D. T. McKean, William Nolte, Vincent Odell, A. J. Oret, John C. Pierce, Jacob E. Phelps, George M. Page, Isaac A. Rice, Murray M. Rogers. Mason E. Rogers,† Francis M. Sherman, George W. Spalding, John M. Schrymer, James Struble, Horace Struble, Aaron Stone, Daniel Smith, William Tanner, Perry C. Taylor, William N. Waldron, D. C. Wright, Francis E. Wheaton,† James H. Wilson, William Walker, Hezekiah Wallace. Musicians—Dighton Phelps, William H. Lawrence, Harry Smith.

Company H, 57th Regiment Pennsylvania Volunteers, commanded by Captain John Griffin, was the second company raised at Athens. This was in the fall of 1861. The following is a list of officers and men at its muster November 25th, 1861 :

Captain, John Griffin ; 1st Lieutenant, Daniel Miner ; 2d Lieutenant, Richard Sinsabaugh ; 1st Sergeant, Joseph Brady; Musician, S. Gibson Shaw; Wagoner, Samuel Marshall. Privates—Mortimer Anthony, Joseph Armstrong, Henry Armstrong, John Burnside, James Brady, James Childs,

‖ Killed at Bull Run.
† Killed at Antietam.

Joseph Clark, Charles Chandler, John M. Chandler, Joseph Clark, George Conrad, Willard Conrad, William Conrad, Francis Conrad, William Drake, Ward Eastabrooks, Lyman Forest, Henry Forbes, Almon Gillett, D. Webster Gore, Samuel W. Gore, Eli F. Hudson, Abram Miller, Milo Miller, Solomon Miller, Amos Miller, Orrin O. Merrill, Charles W. Murray, John E. Moore, John O'Conner, Henry Owens, John C. Parkes, Elmer Phelps, Alvin R. Phalon, William Phinney, Hanford Rolinson, Alpheus Sinsabaugh, Victor Stephens, Orange Shores, Bemer Smith, William Smith, Emery Stickles, Joseph Tripp, Harrison Van Vechten, Levi Anson, Lafayette Anson, Daniel Keeler, William Strickland, Russel Sisson, Edward S. Perkins, Henry Williams, Charles Williams, Oscar Shores, Robert Edmiston, Erastus Green, Hugh Farley, L. Orville Snell, Ezra Spalding, Thomas Dunglass, Allen Chandler, Harrison S. Munn, O. D. Roberts, John H. Rowe, Nathan Gordon, William Wright, John M. Rolfe, Adelbert Hart, Patrick Doherty, Pison Ellis, Merrill McAllister, Harrison C. Perkins, John M. Chamberlain, Thomas M. Guernsay, Joseph B. Evans, John Griffin, James A. Shores, George M. Burns, Samuel Laton, M. D. Mills, George W. Perkins,* Lewis F. Roe, Franklin Shaw, James Wheaton, William Crans, William Decker, James L. Murty, Charles W. Hepburn.

The third company, commanded by Captain J. B. Reeve, was raised in connection with an effort

---

* Promoted to Lieutenant-Colonel.

made at Springfield, in this county, to raise a company. The volunteers of both places were consolidated and formed one company in August, 1862, Company E, 141st Regiment Pennsylvania Volunteers.

The following is a list of the men belonging to Captain Reeve's company : Captain, Joseph B. Reeve ; 1st Lieutenant, J. F. Clark ; 2d Lieutenant, G. C. Page ; Sergeants—Stephen Evans, Tracy S. Knapp, Mason Long, William S. Wright, William Carner. Corporals—Orlando E. Loomis, James W. Clark, Alonzo D. Beach, Charles M. Neal,* William R. Campbell, C. T. Hull, R. Clafflin.† Musicians—W. H. Powers, B. Munn. Privates—H. D. Kinney, Calvin Alexander, James M. Beach, E. W. Baker, Eli R. Booth, Lyman Dunn, Daniel Daines. Melvin Douglass, Aaron Eddy, George Frederick, Wm. Frederick, Abram Frederick, John Frederick, Michael Finney, Truman Galusha, Thomas N. Gilmore, Franklin Granger, Isaac Gillet, John Henry, George Huff, John Huff, Andrew Huff, Lorenzo D. Hill, Matthew Howie, Daniel Hiney, Horace Howe, Russel Hadlock, James H. Harris, George Johnson, E. M. Jackson, John M. Jackson, Charles A. Knapp,* Jac. Lawrence, Alexander Lane, 2d., Isaac C. Lane, William E. Loring, E. P. Lenox, George W. Lord, John Mustart, John Miller, Alanson Miller, Elias H. Merithew, William Miller, James K. Martin, Robert McKinney, Franklin Nickerson, Riley Pruyne, Martin B. Phelps,

---

* Killed at Chancellorville.

† Killed at Gettysburg.

W. D. Powers, Charles H. Packard, George Powers, Edward Price, Levi B. Rogers, George Rogers, Adson B. Stone, William Smith, Orrin D. Snyder, John P. Snyder, John Sanster, Charles G. Sawyer, Charles Tibbetts, Evarts Wandall, W. W. Wilson, Dealmond Watkins, Albert Watkins.

Many other volunteers went from this place and enlisted in the State of New York and other places. Among the number were Henry W. and Augustus S. Perkins, brothers, both of whom joined the 50th New York Engineer Regiment as Lieutenants. Both were promoted to Captaincies. The former was soon appointed aid to General Butterfield, with additional rank, and served with high credit for capacity and bravery to the close of the war, and was honorably discharged with the rank of Brigadier-General. Augustus was killed at the battle of Fredericksburg, in December, 1862, deeply lamented by his companions in arms and by all who knew him.

XXVII.

FLOODS.

SUSQUEHANNA AND CHEMUNG RIVERS.

THESE beautiful streams, one on each side of Athens village, usually flow very quietly by, adding much to the beauty of the landscapes, viewed from the neighboring hill tops. There is in them a succession of rapids and pools, but no dead water, and no unhealthy marshes along the shores. A writer remarks: "That if there be a more beautiful river on the continent we have not seen it. From its source in Otsego Lake, to its union with the Chesapeake, every mile of the Susquehanna is beautiful. Other rivers have their points of loveliness or of grandeur. The Susquehanna has every form of beauty and sublimity." A missionary lady in Oriental Turkey, formerly of this place, writes to an invalid friend, living on the banks of this river: "I should love to sit with you at your window, to hear the voice of the Susquehanna once more. I love that river greatly." The acknowledged healthfulness of this part of the country is attributed in part, at least, to the constant and regular flow of these pure streams.

But these rivers, though so universally admired by strangers, as well as by those who dwell upon their banks, do not always present the same attractive appearance. There are other features at times that are quite the reverse. The melting of the snows and the warm spring rains always swell the streams, sometimes causing a general overflow of the banks, often sweeping away the fences and carrying off trees, the growth of ages, the islands and low grounds being almost literally covered with drift wood. At such times, not only trees and fences, but lumber, and parts of bridges, and of buildings, may be seen floating over the surface, in indiscriminate confusion.

ICE FRESHET.

In the spring of 1784 the inhabitants all through the valley suffered greatly from the sudden breaking up of the ice in the rivers. It had been an intensely cold season, with great quantities of snow. There came an interval of a few days of uncommonly warm weather, which melted the snow in a measure. This was succeeded by severe cold weather, making vast quantities of ice. Warm weather returned again and the waters began to flow. The dams of ice that were formed obstructed the waters, and they sought other than the wonted channels, sometimes overwhelming retired farms, and filling the dwellings with water, followed by the crash of the moving bodies of ice hurried on by the raging waters, destroying everything before it. The suffering of the inhabitants, in the lower part of the valley, from this freshet, was very great.

PUMPKIN FLOOD.

In the fall of 1786, when the crops of corn and pumpkins were still on the ground, continuous rains produced a freshet which has seldom been equaled. The crops were swept away, and the bosom of the river was covered with floating pumpkins. The loss was severely felt, and many cattle died the succeeding winter for want of sustenance. Old people for many years past have spoken of these freshets, the latter being distinguished as the "pumpkin flood."

THE GREAT FLOOD.

But a still greater and more destructive flood, and such as was literally beyond the memory of the "oldest inhabitant," occurred in the month of March, 1865. There was a much heavier body of snow on the ground than usual. The weather became suddenly warm. The snow was in a state of fusion, when a warm rain fell, and the whole came rushing down the hill sides, filling the creeks, and altogether pouring an unprecedented quantity of water into the rivers, suddenly swelling them, not only bank full, but to overflowing ; and almost covering the valley from mountain to mountain, and intercepting communication with either side of the rivers. The village seemed to be almost sinking in the flood. The water found its way into nearly every cellar, and many of them were filled. The foundations of several dwellings were undermined, and fell. On the flats valuable animals were brought into the houses to prevent their being carried down the stream, and many sheep were drowned. One store in the village took fire in consequence of the water coming in contact with lime in the cellar. The upper part of the village was almost entirely inundated. Many left their houses for shelter elsewhere, and many boats were in requisition, to go from one locality to another. The waters of the Chemung and Susquehanna met just below the mile hill, also near the Presbyterian Church, and at the foot of the hill, in the lower part of the village, near the residence of the late Judge Williston, thus making several islands of this village. A view from Spanish Hill, said a spectator, made the whole appear like a great lake dotted with numerous islands. The water was rising for several days, but attained its greatest height on Thursday night, the 16th of March. The citizens were sitting up watching the movement of the water. It continued to rise until eleven o'clock. It then ceased, when, with thankful hearts, relieved of anxiety, the people retired to their beds. The next morning the water was found to have fallen several feet, and many were going about viewing the devastation that had been made.

Great losses have sometimes been sustained by lumbermen on these rivers, by unexpected freshets. Often have their hopes been blasted by the sudden loss of property, the product of many a day of care and toil, and in some instances all that a man possessed has been swept away in a few short hours. But the business of lumbering has often been pleasant and profitable. Most families who have resided here long can call to mind the exciting times of rafting, when pork and beans and bread by the quantity, with ham and eggs, and sundry other luxuries, were in requisition as an outfit for the arks and rafts about to float "down the river." But all this labor was repaid when it was announced that they had found a good market, and that the adventurers were likely to meet the reward of their labors.

It has been remarked as a peculiarity of the Susquehanna, or Crooked river, that nearly all along its course it is receiving tributaries almost as large as itself. It may be added that notwithstanding the much dreaded inundations of spring, with all their disastrous effects, the most of the season the Susquehanna rolls along in majestic calmness, and in mid summer is so low that it is forded in many places.

Some attempts have been made to navigate the river by steam. Two neat little steamboats, the Codorus and the Susquehanna, were launched upon its waters in 1826, and made several trips up and down, much to the gratification of the inhabitants dwelling upon its banks, and the time was anticipated when a regular line of boats might ply upon the river, transporting both freight and passengers. But the want of sufficient water in the low stage of the river soon proved it to be impracticable, and after the disastrous explosion of the boiler of the Codorus, and the loss of several valuable lives thereby, the enterprise was abandoned.

XXVIII.

THE CHURCH.

LESS than a hundred years ago, the region of
country which we inhabit was heathen ground.
The Indians, driven away by Sullivan's army in
1779, were, according to David Brainard and others, "gross idolaters." At Shamokin they had
an idol that Brainard styled "horrible." Before
his conversion Shickelemy, a noted chief, wore an
idolatrous image around his neck. At Queen
Esther's plantation, an officer of Sullivan's army
states that "in what they supposed to be the
chapel, was found an idol which might well be
worshipped without violating the second com-
mandment, on account of its likeness to anything
either in Heaven or earth." At the treaty at Tioga Point, in 1790, while the ceremony of adopting
Thomas Morris into the Seneca Nation was in progress, which was a religious ceremony, the whole
sixteen hundred Indians present united in an offering to the moon, then being at her full. Fish-
Carrier, an aged and noted Chief, officiated as

High Priest of the occasion, making a long speech
to the luminary, occasionally throwing tobacco into the fire as incense.*

The first account we have of any Christian worship in this place, was at the burial of those officers and soldiers in Sullivan's army, who fell in
the battle of Chemung, and were brought back to
Tioga Point for burial. The Rev. Mr. Rogers,

---

* Red Jacket was prominent at this assembly, and no doubt partook of the idolatrous ceremony. He was a pagan, very hostile to
Christianity, and gave orders that when he died he should be buried
after the Indian custom, and refused to allow missionaries to make
an establishment on the Seneca Reservation, in Western New York,
about 1824. Rev. Asher Wright, the missionary who has labored
among the Senecas many years, says: "Red Jacket was a very
intemperate man, and much under the influence of infidel white
men ; and till near the close of his life was opposed to the
Christian religion. A few months before he died he visited an old
friend in Genesee county, who had formerly sympathised with him.
He was greatly astonished at the change apparent in this friend, who
had been converted, and had given up whiskey and was now living
happily with his family. Red Jacket watched narrowly everything
he saw in this old friend, and on his return he said to his travelling
companion: "There must be something better in this Gospel than
I ever gave it credit for if it makes changes like this in men's characters. I should do well to receive it myself. It must be true and
good. I am going to try it." He continued to talk of it after
reaching home, and was in a very serious and tender frame of mind
till attacked with his last sickness. This friend thought that in
heart he believed in Jesus Christ, but he had no opportunity to
make profession of his faith; though he said to his wife, whom he
had once greatly abused on account of her Christian faith, "per-
severe in your religion. It is the right way." This, so far as is
known, was his last utterance upon the subject."

Red Jacket died January, 1831, aged 81 years, and was buried in
a Christian manner, which fact would seem to corroborate the reported change in his views.

Chaplain, preached a funeral sermon on the occasion.

After the Indians were removed the country was rapidly settled by white people from Wyoming and lower Pennsylvania. The Connecticut settlers were of Puritan descent, and were frequently visited by missionaries from New England missionary societies.

Methodist preachers also were early on the ground, classes formed and local preachers appointed.

It was but a little more than thirty years after the heathen left the country, that a church was formed at Athens. One had been formed at Wyalusing as early as 1794, one at Wysox near the close of the century, one established in Smithfield at its first settlement about 1801.

In the fall of 1811, Rev. William Wisner, from Newtown, visited Athens. He was a native of Warwick, Orange county, N. Y., and came to Newtown in 1800. He studied law with Hon. Vincent Mathews, and had practiced at the bar a few years. After he made a profession of religion, his attention was turned to the ministry, and soon after he was lincensed to preach. He came to this place, supposing that the novelty of hearing a lawyer preach might bring the people out to hear him. His subject was "the total depravity of the human heart, the remedy which God had provided for fallen man, and the certainty of the eternal perdition of those who do not avail themselves of that provision." The congregation was large and attentive, so much so that he made an appointment for the next Sabbath, when there were evident tokens of the Divine presence. People came many miles to hear him, and the upper part of the Academy was crowded. A general revival of religion followed. The next summer, on the 8th day of July, 1812, the "First Congregational Church" was formed, with about thirty members, and was connected with the "Luzerne Association." Rev. Ard Hoyt, afterward missionary to the Cherokees at "Mission Ridge," Georgia, presided. While in session, and during the examination of candidates, a middle aged woman from Litchfield township entered the room quietly, and with her usual promptness went directly to the moderator and presented him with a paper. He read it with emotion. It was the certificate that signified the good and regular standing of the aged father and mother, the eldest son's wife, and their daughter Rebecca, in the church where they had lived in Connecticut. Father Hoyt then inquired where they had lived. She replied with a smile, "in the woods three or four miles distant; have lived there about two years." After inquiring if any one present was acquainted with them, and being assured that they were a worthy family, Father Hoyt turned to his brethren in the ministry and said, "Here brethren, the Lord has had a church in the wilderness, and nobody has known it." The church was organized and this family was added to it. They were constant attendants at church; and from their mountain home they might uniformly be seen on the early Sabbath morning in a cart drawn by oxen wending their way down to the landing on the Susquehanna, where they entered their canoe, the aged grandmother, her son and his wife, and sister, and several children, neatly clad in homespun, and floated down the river to the place of worship. After the two services the canoe was entered again, and the boys with their setting poles pushed back to the landing. The old gentleman, blind and feeble, seldom, if ever, came down from the mountain. It was his Pisgah, from which by faith he could view the promised land.

Rev. William Wisner was the first pastor of this church, and remained with it three years, receiving aid from the New Hampshire and Connecticut Missionary Societies. He preached alternately at the old red school-house at Milltown and the Academy at the Point. His instructions were such as to make an impression, and he has been greatly blessed in his labors. Mr. Wisner was eminently a fireside preacher. He went from house to house, calling the family together and conversing with each member. The children shared largely in his attentions, and many a youthful heart was brought to a spiritual knowledge of the Saviour, through his instrumentality. On extraordinary occasions he wrote his sermons, otherwise he preached off-hand. The three years passed quickly, and it was necessary for him to remove to another field of labor.

February 27th, 1816, Mr. Wisner sent in his resignation in the following words :

" Dearly Beloved in the Lord. After striving in vain to retain the endearing relation which has subsisted between us, I do now, with the approba-

tion of the Association and your consent, commit
you to the love of God, and resign my charge over
you."*

After the pastoral relation between the Rev. Mr.
Wisner and the church of Athens was dissolved,
the Rev. John Bascom was chosen moderator, and
Deacon Josiah Crocker, clerk.   Mr. Bascom
preached one-half of his time in Smithfield, employed and paid by the people of that place.   The
remainder of his time was spent in missionary
labors, chiefly at Spencer, N. Y., receiving aid from
the New England Missionary Associations.   The
Rev. M. York, Rev. John Smith, Rev. Simeon R.
Jones, and others, and Mr. Bascom, preached at
Athens at different times, and occasional additions
were made to the church.

In 1818 and '19, a valuable accession was made
of several intelligent Christian families from
Silver Lake, in Susquehanna County.   They had
been induced by the very flattering accounts of
the country to sell their property in New England,
leave their homes and invest their funds in the new
region.   It proved a very unfortunate movement
for them, and they came to Athens in reduced circumstances.   The men engaged as tenants to the

* Mr. Wisner built a house and planted fruit-trees on the lot now
occupied by General Williston. Several of the stately trees are still
bearing fruit.   He was then a little more than thirty years of age.   He
is now near ninety, and is living at Ithaca.   He writes to a friend,
"My life with all its trials has been one of great enjoyment, and I am
happy in the decline of life, as I was in its morning or noon.   God has
not forsaken me in my old age."   Mr. Wisner has often visited here,
and always frequents the old burying-ground, where he finds so many
of his former congregation.

farmers around, and by persevering industry and frugality, with the aid of the little money they brought with them, were carried through the seasons of scarcity which followed.*

But notwithstanding these trying circumstances, that fell with peculiar weight upon these new-comers, the church prospered. It was the practice of the church for many years to meet together once a month, and to bring their children with them to pray for the prosperity of Zion. The Lord hearkened and heard. From 1820 to 1824 there was almost a continual revival of religion. The work of divine grace was manifest in the church, and in the hearts of many others.

At this time the Rev. James Williamson came to Athens. His labors were greatly blessed. There probably was never a time when so happy and prosperous a state of things existed in the church as at this period.

In April, 1823, the Congregational Church of Athens adopted the Presbyterian form of government by a majority vote, to be in connection with Susquehanna Presbytery, originally the Luzerne Association. William B. Swain and George A. Perkins were chosen Ruling Elders.

October, 1825, Rev. Isaac W. Platt was chosen

---

* During these seasons the crops were very short. The people could not wait to go to mill with their wheat, or pay toll at the mills, but pounded out their grain at their homes, and baked it in this crude state. Money was sometimes deposited at the mill to purchase grain, but none could be procured except what was received as toll for grinding. Many sacrifices were made by families to supply themselves with food.

Moderator of the church, and ministered here five years. Many of the church members were not satisfied with the Presbyterian form of government, and at the suggestion of Mr. Platt, the church adopted the plan of Union, recommended by the General Assembly of the Presbyterian Church, and the General Association of Connecticut in 1801. A standing committee of five persons were chosen by the church to act upon this plan, which was generally satisfactory. During the pastorate of Rev. Mr. Platt, in 1826, the first church edifice was erected here. In 1833 Rev. William C. Wisner, son of the former pastor, was called to this church, and remained here more than a year.

Rev. William Adams succeeded him in 1835. He was a man of fine talents and had become quite popular.

About this time a student from Princeton delivered a lecture here upon the subject of Slavery, which created such excitement as to make it prudent for the young man to leave town at the earliest opportunity.

The next Sabbath Mr. Adams preached a sermon against "Popular Violence" which resulted in his removal from this place.

Rev. C. C. Corss became pastor of the church in April, 1837. The General Assembly of the Presbyterian Church, met in Philadelphia, and the following May passed the "Exscinding Act," by which four Synods, 500 ministers, and about 60,000 communicants, were declared to have no connection with the Presbyterian Church, thereby repudiating the plan of Union, upon which ground the

church of Athens then stood. A committee was
sent from the Susquehanna Presbytery to notify
the church members, that they were no longer in
connection with that body, and to organize a church
which should be strictly Presbyterian and in connection with them. The Presbytery was in sympathy with the proceedings of the late General
Assembly.

A portion of the church preferred to remain as
they were, while others chose to be connected with
the Susquehanna Presbytery, thus dividing a small
church. This necessarily involved the question of
church property, which was finally settled by each
body consenting to use the house alternately, thus
causing much that was painful, if not reproachful
to the cause of religion.

Mr. Corss preached for the Old School, and Rev.
C. Thurston for the New School. Rev. Nathaniel
Elmer succeeding Mr. T. This state of things
existed about twenty years, from 1838 to '54, many
hoping for a reunion of the General Assemblies,
which might also unite the churches.

At length during a powerful revival of religion
which occurred about this time, a compromise was
effected, both branches consenting to unite and
transfer their ecclesiastical relations to the Re-
formed Dutch Church.

They remained in this connection until after the
reunion of the two General Assemblies, when the
church again became Presbyterian.

Rev. Augustus Todd, Rev. P. Berry, and Rev.
John Shaw were pastors under this administration.
Within that time the old church was burned in

1861, and a new brick church was erected in 1862.

It is not known that a Methodist class was formed in the village of Athens, until 1832. Mr. Shippy, a class leader lived here, in the early part of the century, and was in the habit of meeting for prayer, with any who might wish to assemble, of whatever name, but it is believed he was connected with the class on the west side of the river, in what was then called "Christian Street," on account of the number of Methodists who lived there. Mr. Abraham Minier was their leader for many years. The street had previously been called Holland, on account of several Dutch families having early settled there. The first Methodist house of worship in the village of Athens, was built in 1844. Dedication sermon preached by Rev. J. Dodge. The church was burnt in 1851, at the time of the great fire, when a number of stores, a long row of buildings, and a small Episcopal church on the bank of the river were consumed.

The Methodist church was rebuilt of brick in 1852.

The Episcopal stone church was built in 1861.

The churches in the upper part of the village, were built some years previous.

XXIX.

MRS. CLEMENT PAINE.

MRS. P. was a resident of Athens many years, and was extensively known in the early part of the century. We have added some account of this excellent woman, with extracts from her diary, which it is thought desirable to insert here as connected with the early history of Athens. She was the daughter of Theodore Woodbridge, brother of the distinguished William Woodbridge, and was born in Glastenbury, Connecticut, September 13th, 1784. The family were educated and intelligent. She finished her education at Hartford in the year 1800, just before her father removed with his family, together with twenty other families, to Salem in Northern Pennsylvania, 90 miles southeast of Athens, which was then a wilderness.

They bought land under the Connecticut title, which was superseded by Pennsylvania claims, but notwithstanding these difficulties they became a prosperous community, one seldom equalled in any new country.

Here Miss Woodbridge commenced a diary which afforded her much comfort in her retired situation, the style and sentiments of her journal would do honor to any of our female writers. Her early reading was principally confined to religious authors of a former period, where she found much to improve her understanding and comfort her heart. Occasionally she visited Wilkesbarre, where she met congenial society, and works of more modern authors. These tended much to her improvement, and although of a very timid and retiring disposition, she could converse and write with uncommon elegance and facility.

In her solitary and retired life she found some valuable Christian society among the people who had removed with them from Connecticut.

After the death of her mother the care and responsibility of the family devolved upon her. Though but seventeen years old she entered upon her duties with fidelity and industry, by which her father, two brothers, and a sister were made comfortable and their home cheerful.

Sometimes in this wilderness the snow was so deep that the roads were impassable, and they saw no faces but those of their own family for many days. While the dreary storm continued, her diary says, "I am by no means discontented, for I have long since been taught that happiness, if anywhere to be found, is in one's own breast, that our own domestic scenes, and our own fireside are preferable to any other. How miserable must that person be who never finds enjoyment at home."

"March 6th, 1804. The storm and cold have

abated, and the spring has returned with all its beauties. I find much happiness in our family. What in this life is there to be compared to domestic felicity. I do not know of a person in the world with whom I would exchange situations." In this peaceful retirement Miss W. often express-es herself as "happily situated," not exposed to the many temptations of more polite and fashionable society. Sometimes she speaks of the cares and responsibilities of the family, sometimes of going into the woods with her brother to make sugar. Sometimes her hand held the distaff, which resulted in a long piece of cloth for family use, and often reading books sent to her by friends, or entertaining missionaries from New England who visited the settlement. Mr. Seth Williston was one of these missionaries, and she regarded him as the instrument of her conversion.

"My good father was overjoyed at the change in my feelings. It has been his highest hope for his children that they might all be brought into the fold of Christ. When the family were assembled for worship it seemed like a little heaven below. Retirement was sweet, and prayer a most delightful exercise.

"There is a work for us to do, and this work is exactly calculated to subdue pride, and remove all self-confidence. It brings us to a state of humility from a sense of our own insufficiency to do any good thing, and that we are forever undone, except God appear for us. When thus prepared God shows the way of salvation through Christ, pardons our sins and gives us faith in Him."

The time came for changes in this retired and peaceful family. Her father married again, and in her diary she writes, "The next year I was united to the man I loved."

Clement Paine was engaged in merchandise at Athens, and purchased his goods in Philadelphia. He frequently passed through Wilkesbarre, where he became acquainted with Miss Woodbridge. He afterwards visited her father's house in Salem, and in 1806 she came with him to Athens as his bride.

Mrs. Paine found some choice society in her new home. Mrs. Tuttle and Mrs. Hopkins, of whom she often speaks as having taken sweet counsel together, were ladies of piety, refinement, and pleasing manners. They often met for social prayer at their own private rooms, and after a little time met at the house (a log-cabin) of a Methodist family to worship on the Sabbath. Here they found the Saviour present time after time, until their hearts became so overflowing that their faith required a larger place. They asked the privilege of meeting in a ball-room on the Sabbath, and invited their husbands to read the sermons, and the Methodist brother to pray. The congregation sang, and they soon collected quite an assembly. Then the Lord directed the Rev. Seth Williston and other missionaries to preach to them occasionally, and afterward a church was formed, and numbers added to it. One of these mothers in Israel, Mrs. Tuttle, lived at Elmira until 1856 when she died. A strong friendship existed between these estimable ladies, which was interrupted by death only to be perpetuated in eternity.

Mrs. Paine had other Christian friends whom she valued highly. In her diary she speaks of her "venerable and much esteemed friend, Mrs. Saltmarsh, the mother of John Saltmarsh, Esq. She is a treasure we must soon lose, as she has passed her threescore years and ten. It was with deep regret that I beheld the decay of her mental powers once so strong, and still less weak than most in the prime of life. How beautiful does that old age appear which is crowned with the wisdom and piety of early days though bowed by infirmity. Such a one is this aged mother in Israel."

Learning the destitution of the Bible about the country, Mrs. Paine corresponded with Robert Ralston, Esq., of Philadelphia, well-known in Bible Society operations, and from him received boxes of Bibles at different times, which with the tracts she procured at her own expense, she commenced a system of Bible and Tract distribution. Long before the American Bible and Tract Societies came into existence, making her way across the rivers and up the mountains on horseback she distributed to every destitute family within her reach. She also employed others to extend the distribution still farther. She was thus in fact the first colporteur in this region.

Nor was this the only way she aimed to be useful. Holding the pen of a ready writer she found access to many others. Her kind and faithful warnings to the thoughtless, and her encouragement to the desponding through the medium of her little notes are fresh in the memory of many. By these and many other methods of usefulness she exerted an influence for good among all classes of society.

The early part of Mrs. Paine's life was tranquil and happy, and she speaks of finding much domestic enjoyment in her new home. She says, "We have all we can wish of riches. We are amply furnished with every thing we need, we have few intruders on our fireside enjoyments; my little Edward every day has stronger claims on my affections, and my husband each day is dearer to my heart."

But her pathway became more rugged as she advanced in life, and increasing cares and responsibilities weighed heavily upon her. Her diary about this time was addressed principally to her children, whom she hoped might be benefited by it in after life. With earnestness does she warn them against the many snares which Satan will set for their youthful feet, and presses it upon them to follow in the footsteps of their godly ancestors, whose prayers are worth vastly more to them than a large estate. Another object she had in view in writing was her own personal benefit and gratification. She loved to call herself to an account, and "talk with her past hours, and ask them what report they bore to heaven, and how they might have borne more welcome news."

March 16th, 1810. She says in her diary:— "Have been very happy in hearing that Esq. Saltmarsh, one of our most respectable inhabitants, has publicly declared his intention of making religion his greatest object of pursuit, and has commenced praying in his family;" and she takes occasion from this example to impress it upon her children to make religion the ultimate purpose of their lives. She warns them against embracing any system that does not exalt God, and humble the sinner, and urges them to see that their views are consistent with the standard of truth by which so many good men have been directed and made happy. "Again, let me entreat you to study the Scriptures with child-like simplicity, and let no persuasions or arguments prevail on you to disbelieve the truth. If you cast that away you are like a ship without a pilot or compass on the wide and dangerous ocean. Be constant in your devotions, at least morning and evening pray for yourselves, for your friends, and for the world. If this is a painful task, pray to God until he makes it a delightful privilege, until he makes you a Christian. Begin a holy life in early days. It is the morning of life and the dew of youth which are particularly acceptable to God. It is then that the passions are most easily subdued. Bad habits and principles are not so stubborn as in later years.

"*October* 28*th*, 1811. Last evening saw an account in the magazine of four young men of handsome talents and acquirements, who had devoted their lives to the purpose of carrying the glad news of salvation to the heathen. I also saw an account of a Mrs. Norris, who had bequeathed $30,000 for the same object. A fear was also expressed that the Missionary funds would not be adequate to the numerous expenses. I was lamenting deeply with Laura that we had nothing to bestow. After many fruitless plans and regrets, the idea occurred that although Providence had not opened a door for us in this way, yet we have an opportunity perhaps of more usefulness than if we had more money at command. There are many children and youth in every village who need religious instruction. Miss Hannah More, by her personal exertions, civilized and moralized a village which previously was extremely vicious and depraved. If we have not, like her, the influence, talents, and education requisite for the establishment of Sunday Schools, yet all of us have qualifications sufficient to enable us to instruct in the simple truths of the gospel. It is also the happy privilege of every Christian mother, to educate a little church for God. Another way in which we may be useful is by prayer."

Mrs. Paine established a Sabbath School in this place in 1818. She often met with the children on the Fourth of July, and furnished them with an entertainment, prepared by herself.

Under date of November 4th, 1811, she writes :— "It is a little more than a week since I heard the distressing news of my dear father's death ! How trifling and little has the world and all its concerns since appeared. It has seemed as if I were but a step from eternity. For a few hours my grief was without any alleviation, until the sweet thought that I should spend a long eternity with him, if like him I lived, darted into my heart. This is as a reviving balsam to my wounded spirit, nor have I since felt my grief so severe. Another great source of consolation is, that this event was the appointment of Divine Wisdom. And shall I repine ? Is it not time that this faithful servant should rest from his labors? His life has been a long and laborious one. Sweet indeed must be his rest. Methinks I see him happy beyond expression, and with his usual tranquil and cheerful countenance, for that bespoke him a saint. I have often thought that his countenance, like Moses', proved that he conversed much with God. His devotions were frequent and fervent. I have heard him relate frequent instances of the efficacy of prayer. He told me one day, that he had been earnestly praying for me, and that God had given him assurance that in his own time he would bring me 'out of nature's darkness into His marvellous light.' This was great encouragement to me, as were his pious instructions. He had a deep sense of the depravity of the heart, and frequently admired the wonderful condescension of God in hearing and answering the imperfect petitions of mortals.

"His charity was bounded only by necessity. On his only visit to me, he saw a widowed mother with her fatherless family. I learned accidentally some months after his departure, that he presented them with $20. A donation of $30, I also heard of his giving to another family in similar circumstances. I am persuaded that many such sums have been secretly given by him, and thus he laid up for himself treasures in heaven which he is now enjoying. His conversation was such as adorned the character of a Christian and a gentleman, and such as pleased and instructed all who heard him. There was an uncommon union of dignity and modesty in his deportment. The vicious feared,

and the virtuous loved him. It was his practice to
do his duty in trying circumstances, and leave the
event to God,—

> ' All the dull cares and tumults of this world,
> Like harmless thunders, breaking at his feet,
> Excite his pity, not impair his peace.'

"He had not a college education, as had his three
older brothers, who were clergymen, yet few have
a better informed mind, or as much taste, judgment,
and sentiment. He became a Christian at the age
of twenty-one ; then he relinquished the company
and amusement of his gay companions, because
they appeared so trifling and insipid compared
with the enjoyments he found in religion. Soon
after, he entered the Revolutionary War, where he
remained during its continuance, and distinguished
himself by his piety and bravery. There he ob·
tained the commission of major. At the age of
thirty-three he married my mother, the daughter
of a rich and respectable merchant. I was their
eldest child ; two sons and two daughters composed
our family. By his industry he procured a com-
petency of the good things of this life, but our
eternal welfare lay nearest his heart. This led him
to seek a residence in retirement, after giving his
children a good education in Connecticut. Three
years after our removal to Salem, my mother died.
During this sore affliction, a kind neighbor endeavored to console me by saying I ought to be
thankful that I had one of the best of parents left.
His character, which I have ever esteemed as the
the most virtuous and valuable that I ever knew,

since his death, shines with increasing lustre. Do you, my children, inquire why he was so justly venerated by all who knew him? I answer, it was piety toward God. It was the approbation of his God which he sought in every action of his life. I wrote to my dear father about two weeks since, and wrote just such a letter as I could wish, had I known it to be my last. Oh, that he had answered it. One request I am glad that I made, it was that he would pray his God to give me grace to bring up my children in the nurture and admonition of the Lord.

"A Congregational Church of eight members had been formed in our peaceful and retired settlement in Salem, but the year after my removal to Athens, God was pleased to pour out his spirit on that place. My youngest brother was from home. My father sent for him that he too might be a subject of the happy work. He saw all his children professors of religion, and every family became a praying family, and, in some instances, four, five, and six in a family became hopeful converts. About forty united with the church. He saw their temporal concerns prosperous, schools established, and the ordinances of religion enjoyed in the place, which in the year 1800 was a howling wilderness. God was pleased thus to smile on his endeavors to be useful. What more had he to do in this world—his work was done, and God took him home. He died suddenly of typhus fever.

"When my sister and myself last parted from my father, he enjoined it upon us, to pray with and for each other. I trust we frequently prayed for each other, but a sinful timidity kept us from social prayer. The injunction came home to us with double force after his death. We have since, each day regularly prayed by turns with the children under my care. I esteem it a great privilege, and it has rendered my sister doubly dear.

"*Sab.,January* 27, 1812. Yesterday I was very happily surprised at the arrival of Rev. Mr. Wisner, formerly a lawyer of considerable eminence, but a change of heart induced him to change his profession. He preached two of the most excellent sermons to-day, to a crowded audience, that I have heard since I have been in Athens. I wonder how any one could remain in unbelief. Sinners must have had their eyes sealed and their hearts hardened indeed to resist the truth. After enduring a long famine of the word of God, it was a precious feast of good things to my soul which I this day enjoyed. He preached in the old Academy, and his text in the A. M., was—'What went ye out for to see?' in the P. M.—'Let us alone, that we may serve the Egyptians.' He showed the wickedness of the Israelites, and the goodness of God, who would not let them alone, and also who they are at the present time that desire God to let them alone.

"I called last evening on one of our neighbors, who is supposed to lie at the point of death, Mr. John Miller, a merchant of this place, about thirty years of age. He leaves a young and interesting wife. I tried to call his attention to the importance of being prepared for death, but his chief anxiety was to know how his widow should be provided for. He died this A.M. and his death was announced to the congregation.

" *Sab., Feb.* 10*th.* In what language can I thank my Heavenly Father for all his favors. He seems about giving his children in this place their heart's desire—in his ordinances and the preaching of the gospel. The Rev. Mr. Williston, Mr. Parker, and Mr. Jones, have frequently preached to us, but they obtained few hearers, and Mr. Wisner came to us with little expectation of doing good. He had, however, a very numerous audience, who were strictly attentive, while he preached the undisguised truth. The second Sabbath, he preached in Milltown to a very crowded assembly, and in this village in the evening. Last Monday I visited at Mr. Crocker's in Milltown, and attended a prayer-meeting. It was with much difficulty I obtained this privilege, yet I found it a happy season to my soul. When I arrived at Mr. C.'s, I I learned he was absent on the business of obtaining a subscription for hiring Mr. Wisner to preach to us a year. How joyfully did we hear the glad tidings that he was likely to succeed, and that the famine of the word we have endured, was to be followed by ' a feast of fat things.' How glad was I to hear that several were awakened to a sense of the importance of preparing for an awful eternity, and to see at the prayer-meeting some children, bathed in tears, earnestly appearing to inquire ' What must we do to be saved.' The little number of Christians are earnestly engaged in praying for the outpouring of the spirit, and for the preached gospel.

"Mr. Wisner returned from Newtown on Wednesday. He proposed a conference which was attended at our house, and I can truly say, it was the happiest one I ever attended. He has made our house his home when in the village, as did the former ministers, and I am thankful for the privilege of entertaining them, and of enjoying the benefit of their conversation and prayers. They earnestly pray for my family. Oh, that their prayers might not be in vain.

"Mr. W. says his way has been wonderfully hedged up whenever he has thought of leaving this people. When he came, he had no idea of spending more than one Sabbath, but the attention the people manifested, induced him to make an appointment for the next Sabbath, and for the same reason he came the third Sabbath. He had with much pleasure contemplated a journey to Ontario, where they were very desirous to have him take the pastoral charge of the church. They had made a regular 'call,' and sent to him, but the bearer lost it on the road, and before it could be renewed he had a pressing invitation from us, and a subscription raised for his support. Last week he remained with us attending conferences, and visiting families, as he found himself too unwell to leave. From these circumstances and the spirit of prayer that prevails, I am led to think the thing is of God."

After an interruption of three years she resumes her journal.

"*Tues.*, *Jan.* 10*th*, 1815. Received a call this morning from Mrs. B—, a temporary resident.

She spoke of the uncommon sorrows which had fallen to her lot. I could not condole with her, for I really could not think from what source her troubles came, as she is a boarder perfectly at ease, has an affectionate husband, and an only son,—a most promising character. I studied much what to say by way of commiseration, but my attempts were awkward. This P. M., another Mrs. B— called. She too spoke of her griefs as if they could not be a secret to any one, yet apparently her situation is pleasant, having a good husband, and an agreeable, affectionate family of children, more than commonly engaging. Next Mrs. H— called. She had not only her own sorrows, but those of her two daughters to bear; all of whom are richly supplied with all this world can give. I thought of my own woes, but had I alluded to them I suppose they would not have been better understood by others than theirs are by me—so I spoke not of them.

"*Thurs., Jan.* 12*th*. Received a visit from Mrs. Shepard, Mrs. Hopkins, and Mrs. Backus. These friends I esteem highly. With the former I have not been intimately acquainted, although a sister in the church, as she has not long been a resident here, she is a woman of a superior mind and pleasing manners.

"*Fri., Feb.* 24*th*. Visited Mrs. —— this P. M. I saw in her family the picture of those who enjoy all the pleasures the present moment can impart, regardless of the future. If all that they now enjoy could be continued, they must have more than the common share allotted to mortals. But their prospects appear to me very gloomy, nothing for a sick day, or old age, and soon they may be deprived of their present very comfortable abode and business.

"*Thurs.*, *Apr.* 20*th*. To-day we have followed Brother Enoch Paine to his long home. After a life of activity, of health, of usefulness, death has laid him in the dust.

"*Sab.*, *May* 7*th*. With all my little ones I attended meeting. Mr. Wisner preached from the text— 'Follow peace with all men.' His sermon in the P. M., was from the remainder of the text—'And holiness, without which no man can see the Lord.' Oh, who could hear what he said, about the consequences of not having holiness, and go away unawakened !

"*Wed.*, *May* 10*th*. Purchased the 'Life of Rev. David Brainerd,' written by President Edwards. If one wishes to know the difference between he who serveth God, and he who serveth him not, let him compare the life of Brainerd with that of the thoughtless and profane.

"*Thurs. Eve.*, *May* 18*th*. Have long had a great desire to read Shakespeare, I flattered myself with the idea of improving my style—therefore sent for the first volume from the village library. I found it was forbidden fruit to me, whatever it might be to others, for the pleasing fiction occupied all my attention, and prevented my search for beauties of style. To my surprise, I found many indelicacies, which I did not expect in so celebrated an author, therefore I shall probably remain ignorant of the beauties of Shakespeare. Oh, that his genius had been better employed! then might those who seek to know Jesus, and him crucified, have known and admired his writings too.

"*Sab., May 28th.* While making arrangements to wait on God in his house, I received an urgent invitation to visit a sick woman. It was two miles distant, and very difficult for me to go, yet I thought it my duty—therefore sent the four older children to meeting three miles distant, took my little one and went to see the sick woman. The family have hardly the necessaries of life, while we have so many of those refinements which sweeten our enjoyment. On our return we called at a house where lives an old man alone. It was old Dr. Dart, he was talking philosophy, and acting it; for with an invited friend he was eating some roasted potatoes on the head of a barrel. He apologized with a very cheerful countenance, said they were eating a very humble meal, but it was the best he had in the house. Poverty, where there is any thing like refinement of manners and mind, does not appear half so disagreeable, as when there is nothing but vulgarity and ignorance.

"*Thurs., June 1st.* The road is filled with travellers going to a camp-meeting about ten miles above us. Some women passed yesterday who had walked thirty miles to attend.

"*Sab., June 4th.* Crowds are still going and returning from camp-meeting. Our family have all attended Mr. Wisner's meeting, and have been richly fed with sweet, divine truths.

"*Sab., June 11th.* Attended meeting at Milltown. The children walked. I never love them so well as when I see them thus presenting themselves before God.

"*Thurs.*, *June* 15*th*. Saw dear brother Bascom, my sister's husband, who brought me the 'Life of Winter' and the 'Life of Dr. Hopkins.'

"*Fri.*, *June* 16*th*. Have heard that Deacon Crocker, who is the chief pillar of our church, is under the necessity of removing from us, being out of employment. This will be a great frown of Providence if it takes place, next to the removal of our minister, which I fear will soon follow if God does not appear for us.

"*Sab.*, *June* 18*th*. Attended a reading meeting, Mr. Wisner being absent, and I enjoyed more than a common Sabbath's blessing in hearing the good Mr. Morse pray. Since meeting, have been much entertained with the life of Winter.

"*Sab.*, *July* 16*th*. What a day of rejoicing has this been to our minister and his church! A degree of that joy which is felt by angels over one repenting sinner has been ours. We rejoice over four who have been admitted to our church. How strong my hopes that this awakening will not end here, that my dear children will also be the subjects of this work. Mrs. W. called to tell me that her son C. W. is under deep convictions. That he spent a sleepless night, he wept much and was in great distress. Should C. become a Christian, what a plant of renown he might be in the vineyard of the Lord!

"*Sat.*, *Sept.* 16*th*. This evening attended prayer-meeting. It was delightful to worship God with the little number of his people after a day of fatigue

and care. I thought how much more delightful it
would be to worship him eternally and without
any mixture of sin. The *eternal Sabbath of rest.*
How delightful and harmonious the sound.

" *Sab., Sept.* 17*th.* Have not attended meeting to-
day on account of the indisposition of my children.
When duty obliges me to remain at home I often
enjoy myself, and find a Sabbath day's blessing.

" *Tues., Sept.* 19*th.* Some remarks having been
made derogatory to the character of another, gave
occasion to our dear minister to say, 'No matter
how true a report is, if we circulate it with a view
of lessening the reputation of the object, it is *slan-
der.*'

" *Wed., Sept.* 20*th.* The ' Luzerne Congregational
Association' is sitting here. I pray that God may
grant them wisdom in all their deliberations.

" *Fri., Sept.* 22*d.* Have felt idle because I have
not engaged in any of my undertakings. My
father used to say that he had rather be driven
with business than have little or nothing to do, and
I have often felt the truth of this remark.

" *Sab., Oct.* 1*st.* This morning I awoke anxious to
attend meeting. If I could not ride, resolved to
walk. As is often the case when I determine to
surmount every difficulty, Providence provided
for me and I rode. I was very much edified by
the sermons, and did not repent my attendance, although three miles from home and five children
with me. With James before me and Seth behind
on one horse I arrived safely. Sometimes I
scarcely know what duty is. I wish to attend the
worship of God with my children. If I cannot take

them, it is my duty to stay with them, as they are
too young to leave, and the difficulty of taking
them is great. We ought to show more zeal for
the worship of God than Christians generally do,
yet to do what appears like saying, 'Come, see
my zeal for the Lord,' does not glorify him.

"*Tues.*, *Oct.* 3*d.* A girl who attends dancing-
school, walks three miles, and crosses the river, and
either has to burden some family with her company,
or return home after ten o'clock at night, last evening
gave me a share of the inconvenience arising from
it. Without any acquaintance or invitation she
called and took tea, lodged, and breakfasted,
thanked me for her entertainment and departed.
I pitied the poor girl much for her folly, gave her
my opinion, intending to spare her feelings yet be
plain. Another case, similar to this, occurred this
evening. It is humiliating to witness the folly of
mankind. Read a chapter this evening to a child
eleven years of age, who said she had never heard
a chapter read before, nor had they a Bible in their
house.

"*Fri.*, *Oct.* 6*th.* This P. M. Mr. Wisner visited us.
While engaged in conversation, a carriage drove to
the door in which were two strangers. It proved to
be Mr. Paine's eldest brother, Dr. James Paine, and
his daughter Charlotte. I had never seen him before, and was never more happy in receiving one
of my own brothers. His prayers and his conversation are a luxury, and prove him a dear follower
of my own dear Saviour.

"*Sab.*, *Oct.* 15*th.* Attended meeting at Milltown.
Mr. Wisner made some remarks, which I applied

directly to myself, and felt very much humbled for my stupidity. Prayers were offered by the deacons, during the intermission, at Mr. W.'s request.

"*Sat., Oct.* 21*st.* Attended prayer-meeting, five only were collected. Mr. Wisner prayed for the outpouring of the Spirit, as if he had the assistance of the Holy Spirit, or as if Christ had met with us.

"*Sat., Nov.* 4*th.* This evening went to prayer-meeting. Saw brilliant lights throughout the village. A humble light shone at the academy where we met for prayer. I felt happy in the idea of meeting dear brothers and sisters. *I met them,* their number was three besides the minister, and what was worse they were just retiring. I had been detained and was too late. I felt ashamed indeed that I should not encourage the heart of our minister by a zeal for the worship of God, and more that I should cheat my own soul of heavenly food.

"*Tues., Nov.* 7*th.* Mr. and Mrs. Wisner made us a farewell visit. We, as a church, deserve the frowns of Providence, and we experience them in the removal of Mr. Wisner, and in the indifference or opposition of our friends and relatives. Mr. Wisner intends preaching here still, but we have reason to fear that his dismission will be the next step.

"*Wed., Nov.* 8*th.* This morning Esq. Saltmarsh was suddenly removed into the eternal world. He was a useful inhabitant and a friend of Jehovah. Oh! that my work of life was done and well done. How sweet would be the sleep of death!

"*Sat., Nov.* 11*th.* Attended the funeral of Esq. Saltmarsh, where was a large collection of people. Heard while at the funeral that Dr. Satterlee, of

Elmira, had mortally wounded himself with a gun that went off accidentally.

"*Tues., Nov.* 14*th.* Have heard the joyful news that Mr. Wisner has concluded to remain with us until spring.

"*Sat., Nov.* 18*th.* To-morrow is our communion day. Had the satisfaction of preparing the sacramental bread. Had sweet reflections while thus engaged, and could say—What am I, and what is my Father's house, that I should do this for the King of kings, my Lord and my God.

"*Sab., Nov.* 19*th.* Our dear minister was ill, and unable to do more than administer sacrament. The affection of this church for Mr. Wisner is very great. Not one of its members would exchange him for any other minister, yet appearances are very dark in regard to his continuance here. The prejudices of the congregation are very great, but not greater than have been against every missionary who has been among us.

"*Thurs., Nov.* 30*th.* This has been our day of public thanksgiving. I did not attend meeting, as the weather has been unpleasant, and the meeting was at Milltown. Our Heavenly Benefactor has done much to gratify our taste as well as to supply our necessities. We partake of the great variety which God has given us richly to enjoy, and although endowed with reason, and capable of all the feelings of gratitude and devotion, yet we rarely exercise them.

"*Fri., Dec.* 1*st.* Received a visit from Mrs. Welles and Mrs. Hollenback, friends and relatives of my early days. Friends and attachments formed at that period are peculiarly dear, particularly when strengthened by a long series of favors, and a continued confidence.

"*Sat., Dec. 2d.* Brother Bascom called to-day. He is authorized by the trustees of the academy to apply to the Theological Seminary at Andover for one who is qualified to teach our academy, and preach to us, as we have reason to fear that our dear pastor will not long continue with us. I find much access to God in prayer when pleading that a door may be opened for his stay with us.

"*Sab., Dec. 3d.* Mr. Wisner preached this A. M. His text was, 'And Jehoshaphat said, Is there not yet a prophet of the Lord, that we may inquire of him? And he said, There is a man whose name is Micaiah, but I hate him, for he doth not prophesy good concerning me, but evil.' Mr. Wisner used arguments which his adversaries could not gainsay or resist. On our return from meeting we called to see an aged lady, Mrs. Prentice, who has probably but a short time to live.

" *Wed., Dec. 6th.* Last evening I was called to sit up with Mrs. Prentice, who was not expected to survive the night.

"*Fri., Dec. 8th.* Mrs. Prentice was buried to-day. She was a woman of good sense and education. She was the daughter of the Rev. Mr. Owen, of Groton, Connecticut. Although more than eighty years of age her faculties were not impaired, and there was still much sprightliness of mind, and gayety of manners apparent. She paid much attention to her dress, and a stranger would not have supposed her more than seventy.

"*Sat., Dec.* 30*th.* Mr. Paine invited Mr. Cook and his brother this evening to supper, they being left alone in their house. Their connection was very singular. Two brothers married the mother and the daughter, and the youngest brother married the mother.

"*Sab., Dec.* 31*st.* Am very much entertained with Miss More's 'Christian Morals.' She has driven me from some favorite, but false notions. Few writers have ever probed my heart so deeply, and exposed its evils so much to my own view, nor has any author ever excited a more humbling sense of my attainments, and of my imperfections. I hope God in his goodness to this sinful world will spare the life, and preserve the mental powers of one so useful.

"*Sat., Jan.* 6*th,* 1816. Attended prayer-meeting this evening. Found no one there but Mr. Richards, nor were any other there but myself and children. Mr. R. sung and prayed, and while I enjoyed the blessing lamented that the ways of Zion should thus mourn.

"*Sab., Jan.* 7*th.* Rose this morning with a desire to attend meeting. Although the weather was disagreeable, I made ready with my children to walk to Milltown. Just as we were on the point of setting out, with some doubts whether we should not suffer from the cold, Mr. R. came in and said he had liberty to take me and the children to meeting in Mrs. Welles' cutter. I could not but think this a kind interposition of Providence, as we must otherwise have suffered, for we had not gone far when it began to snow, and has continued through the day. I did not expect preaching, but just as meeting began Mr. Parker came in and preached, much to our comfort.

"*Wed.*, *Jan.* 10*th*. Had an invitation to an entertainment this evening. Made several excuses, but none would answer, so with a heavy heart I went. My surprise and pleasure were great on finding the party composed of Mr. and Mrs. Wisner with their father, and Mr. Guernsey, the preceptor of the academy. We enjoyed ourselves in rational conversation, but these pleasures will be short, as Mr. Wisner's connection with this church is soon to be dissolved, and we shall be as sheep without a shepherd.

"*Sat.*, *Jan.* 13*th*. Attended prayer-meeting this evening. But two persons beside my own family were present. Mr. Wisner prayed with much fervency for the church in this place.

"*Sab.*, *Jan.* 14*th*. Our dear minister has this P.M. bid a long farewell to Athens—not expecting to preach here again, nor is it thought advisable to have reading meetings at present.

"*Sat.*, *Jan.* 20*th*. Our dear minister has this day removed from us to Ithaca. He bade us an affectionate farewell. When he had gone I wept for myself, and for my children.

"*Thurs.*, *Feb.* 1*st*. Took a ride with my children to Smithfield, to visit my sister. We were all pleased, and loved our little cousin 'Harriet Newel,' Laura's first-born. I felt an affection for it, much like what I felt for my own.

"*Wed.*, *Feb.* 7*th*. Rev. Mr. Smith arrived, and is to preach a short time for us. His society is very instructive, and amply rewards us for whatever trouble or expense we incur for his entertainment.

" *Sab., Feb.* 11*th*. Have been much strengthened in my wishes and hopes of being faithful to my children by two discourses which I have this day heard from Mr. Smith, on these words—' Train up a child in the way it should go, and when he is old he will not depart from it.' He agrees with Mr. Williston, and many other divines, in supposing that God has made a covenant with believers and their seed —that if believers are faithful to their children, he will convert every one of them.

" *Thurs., Feb.* 29*th*. The 'Luzerne Association' meet this week for the purpose of dismissing Mr. Wisner. This is a stroke which will leave our church low. This association is a body of eminently pious divines. A number of them, after their conversion, left lucrative employments, and devoted themselves to the less profitable business of the ministry. Some have had a public education, and the advantages of the ' Andover Theological Seminary.'

" *Mon., March* 4*th*. Had an opportunity of assisting by charity a soldier who had been wounded. His leg had been broken in three places, a ball had remained three weeks in the other knee, one eye lost, one ear cut in pieces, and a sabre wound in the side, in which were taken fourteen stitches. His countenance was very good, and it was gratifying to assist him. If it was done with a right motive, it was a pleasant way of laying up treasure in Heaven.

" *Sat., Feb.* 15*th*, 1817. The cold is very intense.

Mr. Smith says it is the most severe winter we have had for thirty-eight years. There are many sufferers on account of it. The extreme distress it brings, is such as I have never known. Yesterday the cold was really terrifying. The streams being frozen, a famine almost prevails, and I am under serious apprehension that some will actually perish from want. We have baked our last bread, but it is not for myself that I fear. It is for those who have no bread, nor any other comfort, and many such there are around us.

"*Wed.*, *Feb.* 19*th*. Yesterday Mrs. Reddington became the mother of three sons at a birth.

"*Wed.*, *Feb.* 26*th*. Mrs. Gregory watched with Mrs. R.'s last babe the night on which it died. Not one has been spared.

"*Sab.*, *March* 2*d*. Cold, famine, and pestilence seem every day to increase, and threaten desolation. The oldest person of our acquaintance remembers no such time. A mother thinly clad came three miles through the storm, to beg a trifle for her children to eat. I have partially relieved three families to-day. The one best provided for had nothing save some frozen potatoes and milk—a family of nine children.

"*Wed.*, *March* 5*th*. The very great and extreme severity of the weather has abated. It has been remarked by elderly people, that such a severe winter has not been known since the year 1780."

The drought and severity of the weather, of which Mrs. Paine speaks, were felt extensively through the country. The summer of 1816 was very cold. Snow fell for more than two hours on the 3d of June, and vegetation was cut off to an alarming extent.

The drought and scarcity prevailed also through 1817, 1818, and the effects were felt greatly through the winter of 1819. Many families suffered for want of food, and many cattle starved to death. They were frequently found leaning against the fence through weakness, and were often found dead in the fields. The oldest people then living knew of no such time of cold, and famine, and general calamity.

Wells were dry and water scarce. The spots on the sun also added terror to suffering among the illiterate. It was a wonder how the poor subsisted, for the rich had barely the necessaries of life, and provisions could scarcely be obtained at any price. Some nearly perished from cold and want. One family had nothing but damaged turnips. Cold and famine, during the severity of February, 1817, seemed every day to increase, and were sometimes terrific.

Abisha Price was greatly straitened for food for his family, and started out with his gun almost in despair, when he saw a fawn, and was upon the point of firing at it, but discovered that a wolf was approaching behind him. He turned and killed the wolf, then pursued the deer, killed and dressed it, and took it home to his family with a joyful heart. He went to Esq. Saltmarsh, made oath that he had killed the wolf, and obtained a certificate for which he received of the county treasurer twelve dollars bounty. But for the success of this day, he said he could not have supplied his

family through the season with the necessaries of
life.

"*March 8th*, 1817. We have just heard the mournful intelligence, that a little son of Mr. Park was
drowned under the ice in the Susquehanna River."

Not long after a little grandson of Major Flower
was returning home, driving a horse before a sleigh.
They were all found drowned the next morning
under the ice, where they had lain through the
night.

JOURNEY TO BRAINERD.

About 1818 the cause of Indian Missions engaged the attention of many in this part of the
country, and several persons offered themselves to
the American Board of Missions, to be sent as missionaries to the Indians, and were accepted. Rev.
Ord. Hoyt, of Wilkesbarre, was appointed to the
superintendence of the mission among the Cherokees. Soon after a location was made at Brainerd,
on Mission Ridge, about ten miles up the Chickamauga Creek, and a few miles from Lookout Mountain.

Here these devoted missionaries gathered a mission family, of more than a hundred natives, under
their care, with schools, agricultural instructions,
and many religious privileges. The "Mission
House," was built by the president. Mrs. Paine,
possessing much of a missionary spirit, being acquainted with some of the missionaries, and having
a high estimation of the advantages to be enjoyed
there, proposed to her husband, who was in poor
health, to remove South, in the neighborhood of

the mission, where his health might be improved, and their children might receive the benefit of the establishment.   The plan was matured to their mutual satisfaction, and after due arrangements, the family, consisting of the mother, four sons, and a servant girl, with a faithful man to take charge of them, commenced their journey, November, 1820. Mr. Paine attended them as far as Frederick, Maryland, where they expected to meet some missionaries, who were destined for Brainerd. Mrs. Paine's journal says, " While waiting there, Mr. Paine accompanied us to Washington.   We heard the President's Message, and felt grateful for the interest taken in the poor natives.   The address cannot fail to raise him in the estimation of the benevolent.   After returning to Frederick, and not meeting with the missionaries, it was thought best for us to proceed.   Mr. Paine was obliged to return to Athens, that he might settle some secular affairs, intending immediately to prosecute his journey to Brainerd on horseback.

" While at Frederick we became acquainted with the Rev. Mr. Davidson, and heard him preach. One evening the conversation turned on Dr. Boudinot's 'Star in the West.'   Mr. Davidson said he had a friend who had greatly ridiculed the idea, yet wished to read the book, which he did without sleeping, and before half finishing it, became a convert to its doctrines."

It was a favorite theme with Mrs. Paine, that the natives of our country were the lost tribes of Israel.

" We passed through Winchester, and Harper's

Ferry, which Gen. Jones supposes a greater curiosity than the Natural Bridge, appearing to be
built in a large cleft of the rock through which the
river passes.   We saw the Natural Bridge also, so
often described by others.   From a projecting rock
on the north side of it, we had a view of this most
fearful abyss, the bottom and each side of which
are composed of limestone rock, so regularly
wrought, as to lead some to the absurd conclusion
that the whole is a work of art, not of nature.   I
shudder at her temerity, who we were told ascended and turned three times round on a stump,
so near the verge of this awful precipice, that I
dared not go within its reach.   A gentleman described the Otter Peaks, a large pile of rocks on
Blue Ridge.   A rock weighing many tons was
balanced on the top of another ; the surface of this
rock was a space only large enough for two to
stand upon, yet he saw a young lady ascend this
place and dance there.   Is there not a high degree
of infidelity in thus trifling with death ?   We were
willing to believe her the same foolish girl who
performed at the Natural Bridge.   We were much
pleased with the hospitable treatment we received
at the Bridge Tavern.   The blacks at the house
were treated with much kindness, and I was agreeably surprised in seeing one of them reading her
Bible, I asked her where she had learned, she said,
' At the Sabbath-school,' but added plaintively,
' We cannot have them any more.'   I heard this
lamentation from many a poor African.

  "As we approached Knoxville, we met with much
kindness from several families, some of whom felt

much interest in our object. These formed a perfect contrast to the conduct of one family where we spent the Sabbath. The landlord was a weak intemperate creature, and his wife, of course, had the command. They were in good circumstances, but ignorant and profane. The family of blacks were numerous, and had nearly obtained the ascendency. The house was not large, we were obliged to occupy the bar-room. We felt ourselves on more than heathen ground. While the children of the family and the negroes formed a common group in playing ball and swearing, I collected my children around me and we alternately read aloud in our Bibles. I suppose our bigotry, as they would term it, was a subject of ridicule in the early part of the day, but after a time one and another came in to hear a story read, until a small audience of blacks and whites were collected around us. I felt much rejoiced in being able to command their attention, and selected the most entertaining and instructive accounts, and read chapters which described the doom of the wicked. Mrs. W. (the landlady) sighed often, I suppose at the small prospect of comfort in her husband or children which she had in this world or the next.

"When leaving the well-cultivated and fruitful soil of Pennsylvania for the fertile regions of the South, we were greatly disappointed in finding a country comparatively barren—yet we could not but ascribe this and almost every evil to slavery, that bane of happiness and of almost every good principle. There was to me a gloom overspreading each field and prospect, similar to what one might

see in passing through a country desolated by the
ravages of war; only this we might believe transi-
tory, the former permanent. It seemed that the
ground was doubly cursed for their sake, nor was
the curse less discernible on the minds and manners of the oppressors. Idleness, that source of
vice, was a predominant feature. One said to me,
'If you were to live here you would like our
country better than any you ever saw, and slaves
save so much *drudgery*.' True, but this *drudgery*
is generally left *undone!* The remark was often
made that the slaves did not half support themselves. I believe that an income of five hundred
dollars at the North might support a family more
comfortably than fifteen hundred dollars the owner
of twenty slaves.

"We found the poor slaves very grateful for the
least instruction. I asked myself if the perishing
souls of these blacks were not also valuable, and
if these wretched abodes were not *Mission Ground*,
such I was resolved to consider them; here to begin my labors, and to lose no opportunity of tell-
ing them, that they had souls most precious, to be
saved by faith in the Redeemer.

"At one place we saw four small children, the
eldest eight years old and their mother was dead.
These had lately been purchased of their master
for one thousand dollars.

"We saw an encampment of nearly one hundred
negroes, waiting to bury one of their companions,
now in the agonies of death from the effect of
poison administered by one of his comrades with
whom he had a quarrel. The overseer said his

master would not have taken two thousand dollars
for him. We visited the dying man's tent; his
wife and children surrounded his bed in much
affliction. I asked his wife if she thought him prepared for death. 'O yes, madam, through the
merits of our Lord and Saviour, I trust he is.'
She seemed to speak this with the heart and understanding. A poor decrepit gray-headed negro
stood by, I asked him if he was prepared to die,
he replied, 'O no, I don't think I am.' This poor
creature without hope of a happy future, did not
look as if he could survive the fatigue of a journey
to Alabama, whither the overseer said he was taking the crew for trade. One who made a good appearance asked me to walk into her dwelling. This
was the first which did not seem like an abode of
wretchedness. It was neat and fancifully fitted up
with curtains and good beds. She said she had
been owned by many masters, and that all her
children were sold. 'At first it almost broke my
heart,' said she, 'but I am case hardened.' I inquired if there were any Christians on the plantations. She told me of one who was very good,
whom his master and mistress and all loved. Soon
after, I saw the gray-headed negro almost bent
double with age and infirmity, but his countenance
was expressive of a benevolent heart, and peace
of conscience. I said to him, 'They tell me you are
a very good Christian.' 'O no, mistress,' he replied, 'we read there is none good but God.' I
found this poor slave, an intelligent humble follower of Christ. It was most delightful to see
their sufferings thus ameliorated.

"Instances were not unfrequent of mothers being sent from Virginia to Alabama, leaving a family of little children at home, and in these cases they were inconsolable. These bands were generally chained through fear of opposition. In some of them, mulattoes might be seen, said to have been sold by their own fathers!

"It must not be supposed that all alike were wretched; we saw many whose slaves were treated well, were well fed and clothed, yet they cost their owners far more than they could earn.

"A runaway slave had been taken up on the plantation of Widow A., young Atkins came in and said, 'Well, we put the fellow to torture, and he has confessed who his master is. He is a likely young fellow,' said he, 'and we could not think of putting him in jail, as there was one there already who had been taken up for a runaway, and placed there until his master should come, but his feet were frozen, as he had no fire or blanket.' I expressed my horror, regretting that we had passed the jail fifteen miles, and could not leave him one. Mrs. Atkins said this was nothing, that three years ago a black fellow was condemned to be hung for stealing a horse which he rode only three miles, that he was put in jail at Wythe, where he lay during the winter without fire or blanket, and when taken in the spring to the gallows, the blood and water dropped from his legs and feet, which had been frozen to his knees; and his toes dropped off! Fain would I have disbelieved this dreadful story, which was confirmed by two or three of the family.

" One more account shall close this catalogue of
woes. Our landlord in one place related the following :—

"A black fellow on the allowance of only one
peck of corn a week, had been able to split one
hundred rails each day. His master came to him
and said, 'I have laid a bet that you can to-morrow split two hundred and twenty rails, cannot
you gain it ?' He said, 'I do not know, master,
but will try.' He rose early and by great exertion accomplished it. His master instead of re-
warding him with approbation, says, 'I know
now you can, and you shall accomplish this every
day.' He tried but was not able to finish the task,
and was severely beaten. On the third day he fell
short still farther, and was again beaten, with his
short allowance of food, and repeated chastise-
ments, at length he was not able to finish one hundred. His master in a rage approached to beat
him, when the negro seized him by the throat and
strangled him to death, for which, adds our landlord, 'I saw him hung.' I heard many slave-
holders lament that a black had ever come from
Africa. They know not what can be done with
them.

" We had not ceased to travel any day since leaving Frederick, excepting on the Sabbath, and until
within thirty-two miles of Brainerd. Here the rain
had rendered the creeks impassable, and we were
compelled to wait three days. Our host and host-
ess were amiable and 'very kind, but with their
poor management indoors and out, they could
neither make us or themselves comfortable,

though living on a farm which in New England could have supported a family in good style. Their house was without an outer door, or one pane of glass, and unfurnished with shovel, tongs, and-irons, or tea-kettle, with very few chairs, and little table furniture.

"We learned here many things about the missionaries. Our host said they were doubtless the best people that ever came into their country. We were now on Cherokee lands, the appearance of which was very pleasant, there being no under-brush in the woods, and the traveller could proceed without interruption.

"We took leave of our hospitable friends as soon as we could proceed with safety. But we found the creeks much swollen and ourselves in peril several times. I clasped my children in my arms, but could not have saved them had we overset, as the horses could hardly stand in the swift current. Can we ever forget the good hand of our God which carried us through! We spent a comfortable night in a little hut near the creek, and the next night we trusted would bring us to our place of destination.

"We crossed the Tennessee through much danger in a boat which was said to be old and doubtful. The river had not been so high in many years. My fears were wholly allayed by a deep impression of these words, '*It is I, be not afraid.*' After this I enjoyed the sublime scene. We passed the last habitation between us and the mission, but near sunset we found ourselves in a dark forest, the rain falling in torrents to which we were

wholly exposed, and the evil was greatly increased
when we arrived at a high hill, which with much
fatigue and difficulty we ascended. To our great
joy at length we saw a light glimmering on the left.
We had arrived at the consecrated spot. All appeared happy, the doors of each cabin near the
mission were open, in each of which was a blazing
fire, around which the Cherokee boys were playing merrily. We passed by these cabins and entered the mission house, where we were received
with much cordiality and surprise by the family.
We were introduced to a room where was a long
table, around which several well-dressed Cherokee
girls were sitting at work, each with her work-bas-
ket before her. A good supper was quickly prepared, and we were most agreeably surprised in
finding some luxuries to which we thought we had
bid adieu. After this happy interview we retired
to bed. We were led to a chamber neatly furnished, where we found a good fire. All these
things exceeded my expectations, I felt sentiments
of gratitude to the dear missionaries, and was truly
thankful to this great Giver of all.

"I shudder at the recollection of all our dangers,
the more on account of the children, and I love
these young soldiers for their patience and perseverance.

"Having one female attendant and four sons, I
used sometimes to think of Christiana in Bunyan's
'Pilgrim's Progress.' Our sleep was very sweet this
night. The early bell called upon us to rise, and
the bell for prayers summoned us to the dining-
room, and here I had the satisfaction of seeing the

mission family, the precious property of the Christian public and of the American Board. More than ninety interesting Cherokee children were assembled for prayers. A portion of Scripture was read, we heard those children of the forest sing the praises of our God, and bowed with them the knee to Jehovah. The children of the school we ever found most affectionate and interesting, the natives have minds superior to slavery, nor can any tyrant subject them, yet they own many slaves whom they treat with kindness. We found the minds of the children most susceptible of improvement. Religious instruction did not seem like a tale twice told. Their books were their delight, and they seemed to realize their advantages as something new, and which might not always be enjoyed.

"Charles Hicks is well-known as a Christian and as chief of the nation. He had two sons and a daughter in the school. The latter was an interesting, superior girl, her form was elegant, and she possessed much genuine wit, which afforded us all much entertainment. I had the satisfaction of seeing her improve in her temper, which was at first quite ungovernable, and with the utmost joy I saw this dear girl enter an apartment where I was sitting one evening without a light, and kneel down and pray with much earnestness.

"Little Harriet Newel I loved much, she was an interesting sweet child, but easily offended, which she manifested by pouting. I gave her a cake which being broken displeased her. She turned away without accepting it, haughty and straight as an arrow, but reflecting turned with a charming smile, received her cake, and said, 'Mrs. Paine, I will give you my basket,'—her only treasure.

"Wit, beauty, and genius, are not unusual among these children of the forest.

"Delilah Fields I had reason to think was a Christian. I had brought some presents from the school of Miss G. at Athens for the school here. I requested Delilah to write them a letter. One evening she came into my room and said she would write. I gave her pen and paper, but she said 'she did not know what to write.' I dictated the first sentence, and turned to my own engagement. In about half an hour she brought me her letter finished. Very few children would have written as well, for she was not twelve years old. It could hardly be believed that a child of her age who had been at school but two years could write this. It was published in the *Religious Intelligencer*, and I have since seen it in the *Missionary Herald*.

"John Newton was supposed to be a Christian. He was only twelve years old. He was not only loved but respected. There was a degree of dignity in his manners which I rarely if ever saw in a youth of his age. In the coldest mornings when called to prayers, while many of the children were trying to secure themselves a good seat, or wrapping themselves warmly in their blankets, without a choice of seat or a blanket, John Newton, regardless of the cold, with his eyes fixed on the reader, paid the closest attention to what was read and to prayers. He was brother to Harriet Newel. Neither of them had any mixture of white blood. I have often admired their bravery, and their indifference to their food, nor did it afflict them to lose a meal. Excellent fish were plenty, and the boys were fond of fishing. There were formerly no grist-mills in the nation. They are in the habit of hulling corn and making *conahenna*. This is made by pounding the corn, wetting it with lye, then boiling it several hours until it becomes about the consistency of gruel. We could hardly have supported the table without this dish. We also had meat, corn bread and wheat bread, and sometimes a pudding. Our toil was very great, there being but three sisters able to do any part of the mission labor. After my children became inured to the fare of the mission table, they were healthy and contented. They were greatly amused by frequent excursions about the grounds, and much pleased with the hospitality of the Cherokees.

" Marriage is quite customary in their nation, but formerly was but little known. A gentleman from Georgia four years ago passed through the nation, and again last year. He says their improvement as a nation is astonishing. Many of them live in good style. The women spin and the men cultivate the lands. The first class of the men wore fine broadcloth and appear like gentlemen. Ross was a chief, kept a store and post-office. Their connections were numerous and respectable, and lived in brick houses."

Mrs. Paine received some intimation from her husband that the state of his health was such he would not be able to endure the journey as had been proposed. She writes, "Mr. Paine began his journey to Brainerd, but was unable to prosecute it, which rendered our return necessary. A man was sent commissioned and prepared to remove myself and children again to Pennsylvania. There was no doubt in the minds of our pious friends at Athens, there was no doubt in the minds of the missionaries, nor could there be any in my own mind as to the duty of returning. We left the mission, April 3, 1821, with feelings of the deepest regret, which could only be soothed by the prospect of meeting a husband and a father. The missionaries and the children affectionately assembled in the piazza where a prayer was made, and a parting hymn sung. We took leave of the children individually, some of whom wept aloud.

"Mr. Paine expected if his health admitted to meet us in Virginia. Our expedition was greater than we had anticipated, and it was not until we arrived in Pennsylvania, on the first of May, that we saw him pensively riding down a long hill, and fording a river, without observing us, until one of the children grasping his hand says, 'Pa, we are all here.' Merciful Father, how great was thy mercy and goodness which enabled us to say, 'We are all here.' "

Mrs. Paine's life was that of a uniformly devoted Christian, always watching for opportunities for usefulness. Even after her hand was palsied in her last sickness, she commenced a note to a friend, which she could not finish, recommending an object for the benefit of youth, that would be elevating and instructive. But the map of the Celestial city was ever before her, and when the messenger called for her to go thither, she was not surprised.

She calmly said, "I have done with the world, I have nothing more to do. To look back, all is darkness, but," pointing upward, "yonder, yonder, up there, all is bright, beautiful, beautiful. There is the Father, Son, and Holy Ghost."

Death is welcome to those who have nothing to do but to die. She closed her mortal existence, Oct. 6, 1834, in full faith in the Resurrection. "Christ the first fruits, afterward they that are Christ's at his coming." A beautiful poem she wrote on this subject, some years before her death, may be appropriate to insert.

THE RESURRECTION OF A GOD.

TWICE had the sun in darkness left the world,
And twice had night her sable robes unfurled,
And anxious nature in suspense yet stood,
Death held his sceptre o'er the Son of God!

The hours in solemn silence passed away,
The guards were waiting the approach of day,
The midnight moon gleamed on the extended spears,
Their helmets still reflected back the stars.

At length the day-star blushed around the east,
And cast her beauteous beams on distant west;
Sweet morn once more dispelled the gloom of night,
The azure sky again was dressed in light.

When, lo! convulsions shake the solid ground,
Spreading confusion and dismay around!
A glorious angel swift descends from heaven,
The guards fell backward, from his presence driven!

His face divine beams with immortal glow,
His form celestial, garments white as snow;
The seal was broke; the stone was rolled away,
Angelic guards the wondrous work survey.

The seal of death was broke, the work was done,
The angel sat upon the ponderous stone ;
Death from the sepulchre shrunk back to hell,
The awful news of ruin there to tell !

But who is this, arising now, comes forth
In robes of blood and garments dyed in death ?
In awful majesty, lo ! see him come
Divine and lovely from the yielding tomb.

O Zion ! 'tis your king—ye Christians tell,
This is your God, who broke the powers of hell ;
For you, the wine-press he hath trod alone,
For you, the vengeance of his God hath known !

And now behold the resurrection morn,
Angels behold the first of nature born !
He rises conqueror from the cruel grave,
He comes, O guilty man ! with power to save.

Ne'er did the world behold the rising sun,
In glory thus victorious return ;
The morning stars with joy together sang,
The echoing sound o'er heaven's wide concave rang.

The God of mercy from his throne looked down
Well pleased that through the atonement of his Son,
He could be *just* and on redemption's plan,
Save guilty,—ruined—yet still favorite man !

Soon shall the deserts blossom and rejoice,
Soon will the nations raise their tuneful voice ;
From distant heathen lands—from shore to shore,
The Babe of Bethlehem sing—the triune God adore.

ATHENS, August 7, 1829.   A. P.

NOTE OR CONCLUSION.

There are doubtless many interesting facts connected with the history of Athens that have not come to the knowledge of the writer.

It is not claimed that the record is all that could be desired ; it is hoped, however, that it may aid in a future and more complete history of the country in this vicinity, whenever another hand shall undertake the task.

NOTE.—Chickamauga was a reservation of the Cherokee nation, containing twelve thousand square miles, guaranteed to them by the United States government; two-thirds of which lay in the northwest part of Georgia. Brainerd, the first missionary establishment of the American Board among the Cherokees, was made in 1817, on what has been since called Mission Ridge, much noted in the late war, and within the bounds of the reservation, with farmers, mechanics, physician, and teachers, to instruct the natives, and introduce among them habits of industry and civilized life.

The mission was in successful operation, until the laws of Georgia were extended over them. Two of the missionaries were imprisoned for refusing to take the oath of allegiance to the State of Georgia. They were taken from their fields of labor, by armed soldiers, and immured in the penitentiary for a year and four months.

The lands of the Cherokees were surveyed and divided into farms, and distributed by lottery among the inhabitants of the State. The United States also took the 8,000,000 of acres of land, paying them the sum of 500,000 dollars, and removed them beyond the Mississippi. Such were the hardships they endured when journeying to their new homes, that one-fourth of them died on the way.

They were removed across the Mississippi in 1827, '28, and '29, numbering more than 20,000 when they left Georgia. Many of the missionaries went with them. They are now called a Christian nation. —*Vermont Chronicle.*

NOTE—Near the close of the late war, a gentleman from Chicago with two officers from Chattanooga, visited the old Brainerd Mission Station on Mission Ridge, seven miles east of Lookout Mountain. The mission-house and mill are still remaining. In a clump of trees near by is the old mission grave-yard. The monument of Dr. Worcester, whose dust has been removed to New England, is in a state of preservation, and the inscription plain. He died while on a visit of kindness to the Cherokee people.

Mr. Vail, who went as a missionary farmer in 1819, is the only remaining representative of the mission, now living near Chattanooga, and is an elder in the church at that place, the church being composed, in part, of members from the original Congregational Church at Brainerd. The gentlemen were greatly interested in Mr. Vail.—*Missionary Herald,* 1866.

APPENDIX.

In 1828 Colonel John Franklin, of Athens, Pennsylvania, prepared a series of articles, which were published in the *Towanda Republican*. The number for February 14th of that year, containing the account of the Battle of Wyoming, will no doubt be read with interest, coming from that remarkable man.

As I was living in Huntington, upwards of 20 miles from Wilkesbarre, from the 1st of June, 1777, to the 3d day of July, 1778, and although I can state the facts, I cannot name the dates of all those transactions.

The inhabitants in their respective districts erected forts to resort to for defence in case of an invasion. Two forts were erected in Exeter, one at Wintermoots, and the other at Jenkins, at the Lackawanna ferry. Some time in June two or three men were murdered up the river above the forts in Exeter, by Indians or Tories. Application was then made to the Board of War for Capt. Spalding with his company to be sent to Wyoming to defend the inhabitants; orders were given for that purpose. The company was at that time with a Pennsylvania regiment at or near Valley Forge, when the orders were received for them to return to Wyoming. But probably from the influence of Pennsylvania Tories, or others who were opposed to the inhabitants holding the country under the jurisdiction of Connecticut, or as was suspected from some evil design, the company was not permitted to return immediately to Wyoming, but were kept with the regiment and marched a different course for several days and were finally discharged at Lancaster, from which place they marched for Wyoming, and arrived at Shoop's Inn, in Northampton County, about 30 miles from Wyoming, on the evening of the 3d of July, the day on which the massacre took place. Had they not been thus detained, they would have been at Wyoming at least six days before the battle was fought.

Having satisfactory information that an army was on their way to invade the settlements, Cols. Butler and Denison, with six companies of militia, and Capt. Hewit's company, marched some distance up the river the last day of June, with a design to meet the enemy and attack them before they reached the settlements below, but returned without discovering any except two Indians who, having their retreat cut off, attempted their escape by swimming the river. Lieut. Roswell Franklin and another person pursued them with a canoe, and dispatched them with their setting poles in the river. It appeared that the body of the enemy, to prevent being discovered, had marched through the woods back of the mountains some distance from the river settlements. It was well ascertained that the Wintermoots and some others had driven cattle over the mountains to feed the enemy when on the way. Having ascertained that the enemy were not far distant, the inhabitants resorted to their respective forts with their women and children; those in the neighborhood of Wintermoots resorted to that fort, where Daniel Ingersoll who resided in the neighborhood took the command.

On the first day of July, two of the Wintermoots left their fort and went over the mountain on pretence of making a discovery; they returned to the fort very quietly in the evening, and called for entrance. The gate was opened, when the villains led Col. John Butler with his army of Tories and Indians into the fort, and the few innocent families who had resorted there for safety, were made prisoners. On the morning of the 2d July, a detachment

of the enemy marched to Jenkins' fort where the few
families in that neighborhood had resorted for safety, not
being able to defend themselves, surrendered, and the
enemy took possession of the fort and made prisoners of
its inmates.

July 2d, at nine o'clock in the evening, I was in Huntington, a mile from home at a neighbor's, when I received
by an express the following letter :—

"KINGSTON, 2d of July, 1778.

"To Capt. JOHN FRANKLIN.—Sir, you are commanded to
appear forthwith, with your company, at the Forty fort
in Kingston. Don't let your women and children detain
you, for I don't think there is any danger at present, for
the enemy have got possession of Wintermoots fort, and
I conclude they mean to attack us next. You will act as
you think prudent about ordering the women and children
to move to Salem ; but you must not wait one moment to
assist them.

"NATHAN DENISON, *Colonel.*"

"To Capt. WHITTLESEY,

"You are desired to forward the above with all possible
expedition ; don't let any thing detain this—Press a horse
if needed.

"NATHAN DENISON, *Colonel.*"

My company lived scattering—a part in Huntington
and the remainder along the river from Shickshinne to
near Berwick—the greatest number however lived in Salem. The letter was copied and sent to my lieutenant, Stod-
dard Bowen, at Salem, with directions to have him meet
me at Shickshinne early the next morning, with all of the
company that could be collected in that quarter ; notice
was also given to every family in Huntington. Two of
the company from Huntington were at that time in Shawney, and three at Shickshinne.

Early in the morning July 3d, I took my family to a neighbor's house where I met with six men, all that could leave Huntington with safety to the women and children. We marched to Shickshinne. Lieut. Bowen had been there, and taken with him three men who were there, and had been gone an hour; he had left a sergeant to collect the men in Salem and follow him. We had gone but a short distance when we met an express (Benj. Harvey) with a letter from Lieut.-Col. George Dorance, informing me that "the Tories and Indians, about 600 in number were in possession of Wintermoots fort—that he expected they would attack Kingston next, and requested my assistance, with my company, with all possible speed." He had also written a few lines to a Capt. Clingman, who was then stationed at Fort Jenkins, near Fishing Creek, with 90 men, requesting his assistance with his company at Kingston. I also underwrote a few lines to the same purport.

When we reached the garrison at Shawney, we had information direct from Kingston, that Cols. Butler and Denison, with all their forces had left the fort and formed a line at Abraham's Creek a short distance from the fort, and did not expect an attack from the enemy until the next morning. From that information I left part of the men I had with me to wait a short time for the arrival of the residue of the company from Salem. I marched on with four others, and when we came opposite to Wilkesbarre we heard the firing, not heavy but scattering. We hastened on with all speed, and found on arriving at Kingston fort that a battle had been fought, and Cols. Butler and Denison, with 15 or 20 others had in their retreat gained the fort. Col. Butler tarried there but a very short time, when he crossed the river to Wilkesbarre. From Col. Denison and others I got the following particulars.

The enemy having possession of the two upper forts,

it was expected they would attack Kingston next. Five companies of militia, to wit : three from the east side of the river and two from the west, with Captain Hewit's company were collected at Kingston fort.   In consequence of the enemy being in possession of the upper forts, no assistance could be had from the inhabitants in that quarter. The enemy had taken possession of all the water craft at Jenkins' ferry so that the Lackawanna company commanded by Capt. Jeremiah Blancher, had no way of getting to Kingston unless by going down on the east side of the river and crossing at the fort, and leaving their families behind where they might have fallen an easy prey to the enemy.

The precise number collected at Kingston fort was not ascertained, I am, however, confident from my own knowledge that the whole number, including Capt. Hewit's company, did not exceed 300 men.   I knew every man that was in the battle from Shawney ; their whole number was only 44 ; a small number from each company was left in their respective forts to guard the women and children.

On the morning of July 3d, Daniel Ingersoll, then a prisoner in Wintermoots fort, was sent by Col. John Butler, commander of the enemy, with a flag to Kingston fort, proposing to Cols. Butler and Denison that on condition of surrendering without bloodshed, he would give them good terms of capitulation ; a surrender was refused and the flag returned with information accordingly.

After the flag returned, Cols. Butler and Denison, with all their forces left the fort and formed a line at Abraham's Creek, with a view of attacking the enemy before they reached the fort ; that in case they were not able to hold their ground they could retreat to the fort.   Capt. Mc Carragan, of the Hanover company gave up the command to Capt. Lazarus Stewart, an old warrior, and went with him. Lieut. Lazarus Stewart, Jr., went on as a volunteer in the same company.

Some short time after the middle of the day, it was discovered that the enemy were burning all the settlements above, and collecting all the cattle within their reach; but from appearance it was apprehended that they would not risk an attack upon Kingston, but would burn, plunder, and destroy all the upper settlements, and would probably cross the river to Lackawanna, and take possession of that fort, destroy the settlement, and probably massacre the people or make them prisoners and return back with their booty from whence they came. To prevent which it was proposed by some of the officers to go and attack them on their own ground, which was finally agreed to, though reluctantly by some. Col. Denison informed me that he said as much against it as he could say, without being called a coward. It was his wish to wait for more strength—for the arrival of my company, which he expected would be on the following morning, and further for the arrival of Capt. Spalding's company, as Lieut. Timothy Pierce, arrived with information that the company were on the way, and would probably arrive on Sunday for their assistance; but fearing that it would then be too late, that the enemy would draw off with their booty before any further assistance could be had, it was determined to attack them.

Capts. Durkee and Ransom, Lieuts. Ross and Welles, with a select party marched forward as the advance, and formed the line of battle; Capt. Hewit's company on the right, and Capt. Whittlesey's company on the left. When they came in sight of the enemy, they were in a body about Wintermoots fort; but they instantly formed a line across the plain, covered with trees and brush to a swamp on their right. Cols. Butler and Denison with their small forces advanced to a line drawn for action, to meet the enemy, who were at least double their number. The battle now commenced, and the firing was heavy for about 30 minutes; the left wing of the enemy was forced back, and Capt. Hewit's company and others on our right wing had gained about 30 rods of ground, the enemy breaking before them. Our left wing held their ground, and victory over our enemies was considered sure, when it was discovered that the Indians were advancing round in the swamp to surround our left wing, when orders were given to flank off to the left to prevent being surrounded; but through mistake it was said that orders were given to retreat off to the left, and some person (probably through fear), cried out that Col. Denison had given orders for the left wing to retreat—they gave back, and the Indians set up a hideous yell and advanced. Attempts were made by the officers to prevent retreating, and to bring them up to face the enemy and to stand their ground, but in vain; the word "retreat," though not intended, proved fatal—a general retreat taking place. The left wing first giving way, when the right wing was advancing, their retreat was cut off by the bend in the river below. The savage Indians, and Tories of a more savage nature, rushed on with their guns and tomahawks; the slaughter became dreadful; the greatest number that escaped the slaughter was by crossing the river; numbers were killed in the river in attempting to cross, numbers surrendered on the promise of good quarters—in one particular case about 20 got into the river in company, where they were fired upon by the Indians and Tories, and several were killed, when they proposed to the survivors that if they would come to shore and surrender themselves they should not be injured— that their lives should be spared. Trusting to these promises, 15 in number returned back to the shore and surrendered themselves prisoners; they were led off some distance to the road, where they were set down in a ring facing each other, with an Indian to the back of each one, to hold them down, when the old squaw, Queen Esther, followed round the ring to the right with a death maul, with which she broke their skulls. Among these prisoners was William Buck, a lad about 15 years old, a son of Lieut. Asahel Buck; he was not held, and seeing the old squaw killing the prisoners, with her death maul, he started and ran off crying; he was pursued by an Indian who took him, and flattered him that as he was a white-headed boy he should not be hurt. But while he was leading him up to the ring, another Indian came behind him and struck a tomahawk into his head and put an end to his life. Lebeus Hammon, being a stout man, a large Indian stood behind him with his hands on his shoulders to prevent his rising, seeing but one man on his left to receive the fatal blow before his turn should come, he concluded that he could but die, and that he might as well make an attempt to save his life as to sit still and receive the fatal blow from the death maul of the old Queen, gave a sudden spring—arose from the ground and knocked the Indian down that was holding him, ran into the woods, pursued by two Indians, but turning one side from his course under cover of a tree, and a bunch of brush, the Indians ran by a short distance, when he changed his course through the woods and escaped with his life. The other fourteen were killed, stripped and scalped, and left lying in the ring with their feet towards each other.

I was informed by a man who escaped the slaughter, that a man of the name of Calwell, in Capt. Whittlesey's company on the left wing, was killed in the commencement of the action, and that he was the only one of that company that fell until they commenced their retreat. And from the best account that could be had from those that made their escape, and from examining the ground, the greatest number that were slain had surrendered themselves prisoners on the promise of their lives being spared and were afterwards inhumanly massacred.

LAND TRANSFERS.

The following is a record of the transfer of certain lots of land in the village of Athens.

TITLE—1789—APRIL 13TH.

Solomon Bennett to Andreas Budd, the grantor for value received gives up all his right and title to a certain lot of land lying on Tioga Point, known as Number 6, containing nine and three-quarters acres.

TITLE.

John Franklin to Andreas Budd, 30th March, 1793; consideration, three pounds.

Right of lot of land lying and being in Athens aforesaid, and being in that part of said Athens called the town plot, and being lot Number 40, the first division of lots in said Athens.

Said lot bounded northerly, on a piece of land laid out for public use; westwardly on a highway laid out through the town plot; eastwardly on Susquehanna River. Said lot being 6 rods wide on a north and south line.

TITLE.

Andreas Budd to Elisha Mathewson, 17th June, 1795, conveys both these lots for eighty pounds.

Index